Workshop Devices

Robert Wearing

HarperCollins*Publishers*

First published by Evans Brothers Limited 1981
First published in paperback by Bell & Hyman Limited 1984
Revised edition published by Unwin Hyman London 1987
First published by HarperCollins Publishers London 1991
Reprinted 1992, 1993

ISBN 0 583 314627

Illustration by Gay Galsworthy

Printed and bound in Great Britain by Cox & Wyman,
Reading, Berks

This edition was specially produced for Traditional
Woodworking by arrangement with HarperCollins Publishers.

HOLDING
DEVICES

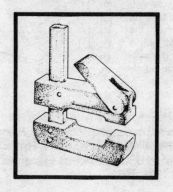

1 Improved sawing board

Fig.1

This board has several advantages over the conventional bench hook, particularly for the beginner and the inexperienced. The board itself is held in the vice thus eliminating one cause of movement. In this position the work can be firmly held with a cramp, further preventing movement. The sawing position is thus similar to the planing position.

2 Rebated vice jaws

If the basic vice jaws are rebated at their ends, as the illustration shows, quite a variety of useful and helpful auxiliary jaws can be instantly fitted. In a communal workshop it is important that these jaws be accurately and identically machined.

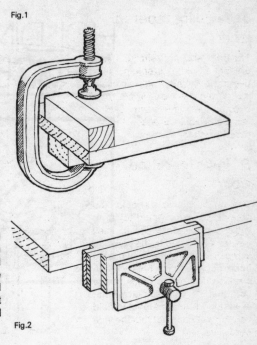

Fig.2

3 Carpet jaws

Good quality 13mm (½in) plywood makes a good backing for these jaws. It is advisable to machine an ample length of rebated hardwood strip to make the sockets. The sockets are glued on with a rebated jaw in place, using a thickness of card to give an easy sliding fit. Jaws lined with clean carpet offcuts are most useful for holding polished and well-finished work. Great care must be taken to keep these jaws free of glue.

Fig.3

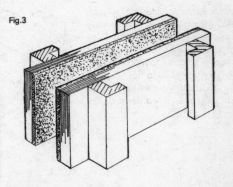

4 Jaws for tapered work

Tapered legs and similar items present a holding problem easily overcome by this single auxiliary jaw. When the taper is cut on a circular saw, the same setting can be used to produce the tapered block for this jaw.

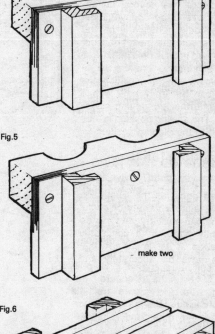

Fig.4

5 Jaws for round work

The two blocks should be cramped or even glued together while the holes are bored. They can then be glued to the plywood in the vice, round material having been inserted in the holes. When marking out for the holes, make sure that they are so placed that when long round material is held vertically, it does not foul the vice slide bars.

Fig.5

make two

6 Cradle jaws

The traditional planing cradle does not hold the work very firmly. The cradle jaws do. They are particularly useful in planing octagons prior to turning or using with rounders, also for planing flats on round material, for example to receive mortises.

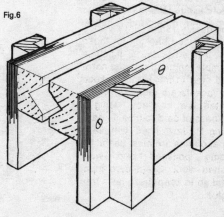

Fig.6

7 Leather-lined jaws

These jaws are particularly useful for holding backsaws, small handsaws or scrapers for sharpening. They hold the job firmly and reduce the unpleasant noise which is unavoidable when filing saws.

It is advisable to protect the workbench from metal filings with pieces of paper or a plastic sheet.

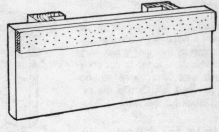

Fig. 7

8 Single tall jaw

This will be found to have several uses. **A** The tall jaw will hold a wide board firmly against a pinned or screwed strip for planing. **B** Squaring wide boards with a knife provides a basic difficulty. The large square tends to drift as the knife runs against it. By pulling firmly on the try square stock both work and square are held firmly against the tall jaw. Squaring at the other end is accomplished by an overhand grip, knifing away from the operator. **C** A block held in the vice is another alternative.

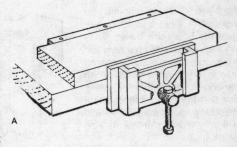

A

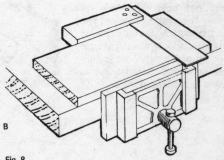

B

Fig. 8

9 Sash cramp holder

A convenient way to hold small boards for face planing is to grip them by the ends in a sash cramp which in turn is held in the vice. The plan view **B** shows this. The cramp jaws must, of course, be below the surface to avoid damage to the plane cutter. This jaw arranged similarly to Fig. 3–7 neatly grips the sash cramp bar at one of two heights to suit differing thicknesses of work. The two rebates together must be less than the thickness of the cramp bar.

10 Shooting mitres

Mitres can be shot with this jaw as long as not too great an accuracy is required. The back board is similar to earlier examples and to it is fixed a hardwood strip of about 20 × 13mm ($\frac{3}{4}$ × $\frac{1}{2}$in). The work is gripped firmly against the stop piece while being planed. As long a plane as possible should be used so that a good part of the sole can rest on the bench top.

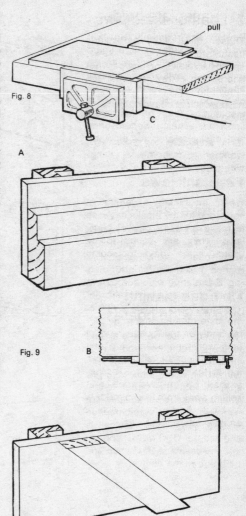

Fig. 8

Fig. 9

Fig. 10

11 Faceplate holder

Bowl turners frequently require to work off the lathe using a sharp scraper on difficult or torn areas. A pair of jaws as illustrated enable one to grip the iron faceplate on which the bowl is mounted. It can be held very firmly while being worked upon and easily rotated for convenience.

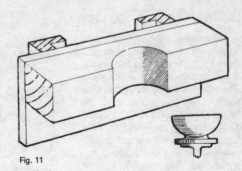

Fig. 11

12 Blank jaws

When machining a length of hardwood for the blocks it is wise to make an extra pair of blank jaws. They are bound to be useful some day for some purpose.

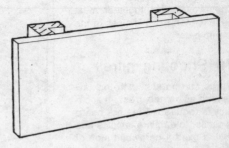

Fig. 12

13 Edge planing of long or wide boards

The bench vice holds one end securely, the other end needs support. **A** and **B** show the method when the inner vice jaw is flush with the bench edge. When the vice is not so fitted, for example with the recommended rebated jaws, the device is modified to **C**. Two G cramps hold the device to the bench and the board to the device.

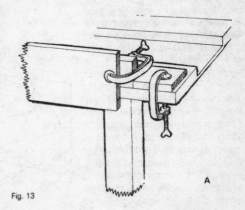

A

Fig. 13

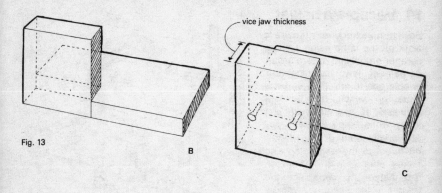

Fig. 13

B

vice jaw thickness

C

Fig. 14

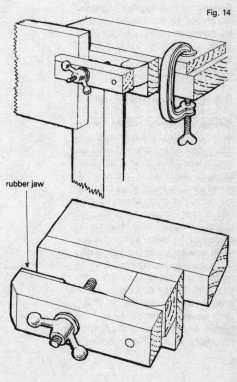

rubber jaw

14 Long board holding device

A further improvement for benches with the recommended outstanding jaws is modelled on the handscrew principle. The baseboard cramps to the bench top with the inner jaw overlapping the edge. This carries a curved spacing block of about 25mm (1in) thickness, into which a short dowel is fixed. A thread of about 10mm (⅜in) with wing nut and tommy bar operates the jaw. It is an advantage if the jaw is lined with rubber, for example an offcut of rubber webbing.

15 Mortising block

Fig. 15

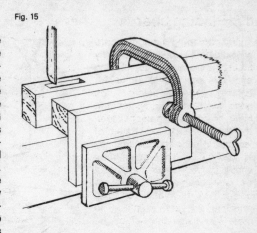

It is bad practice to mortise in the vice as the workpiece can be scratched through sliding downwards through the jaws. The vice can be used, however, to grip the mortising block as shown. The work is held to the block with a G cramp or handscrew. This holds the workpiece firmer than cramping direct to the bench top and makes sure it is truly vertical. The thinner the workpiece the greater is the security given by working by this method. Alternatively, the block can be held to the bench top with two long bolts and wing nuts.

16 Planing boards

This is the simplest of a number of planing boards. Shaped work always presents holding problems, particularly thin pieces. A stout block is gripped in the bench vice. The board itself may be solid wood or blockboard. A small amount overhangs the vice jaw with the bulk sitting on the bench top. Buttons of hardwood, slightly thinner than the workpiece, and fitted with countersunk screws, hold the job firmly, **A**. A further improvement is to replace the buttons with circular cams, **B**. These can be turned to a diameter of, say, 35mm (1⅜in) then sawn off and drilled well off centre and countersunk. A 6mm (¼in) hole takes a No. 12 screw.

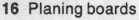

A

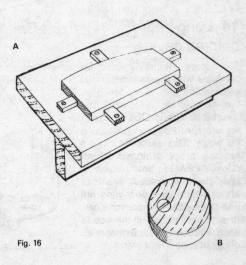

Fig. 16

B

17 Planing boards

This boomerang type of board will hold both parallel and slightly tapered components for planing and it is particularly useful for holding thinnish pieces. The edge strip and the boomerang must, of course, be thinner than the workpiece. An assortment of lengths, widths and thicknesses is desirable. The boomerang should be of multi-ply and should be well countersunk to avoid damage to the plane iron. The principle is very simple. The more you push, the tighter the grip.

The boomerang can be screwed to the bench top and used with a tall auxiliary jaw as in Fig. 8, or a piece standing above vice jaw height. In this case it is advisable to drill a line of 6mm ($\frac{1}{4}$in) holes about the same depth 6mm ($\frac{1}{4}$in) and about 25mm (1in) apart. This avoids projecting roughness on the bench top caused by the screws.

18 The lever cam clamp

The use of cam blocks on a holding or planing board has already been described, Fig. 16. This variation is frequently found to be better and more convenient. Make them from stout plywood and drill eccentrically. **B** shows a typical shape.

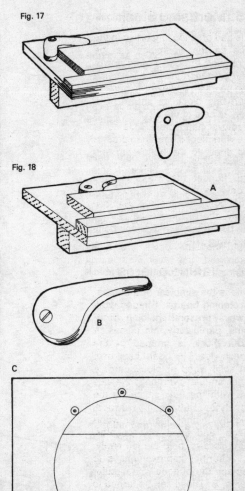

Fig. 17

Fig. 18

In **A** a small board is shown being held on a planing board between a lip and a lever cam clamp. Screw the clamp on so as to grip on a smaller radius. Pulling in the lever increases the radius at the grip point. Make sure when fixing that the lever cam clamps even more tightly if the workpiece moves forward.

This device has also been used successfully in gluing up a small circular table top which had split, **C**. Use a 20mm (¾in) blockboard or chipboard base, a few basic circular cams, Fig. 16B, and, say, three lever cam clamps. Providing that the cams are firmly screwed, the lever clamps will bring the joint together and hold it firmly.

19 Clamping sawing board

The sawing board illustrated was designed for a handicapped student having the use of one hand only. The ideal clamp is one of the fast-threaded wing nuts, alternatively a screw and nut must be modified from standard patterns. Backflap hinges secure the clamp plate to the angled rear block. The screw position must permit the gripping of material 75mm (3in) wide. A jaw made from a piece of so called half-round moulding 25mm (1in) nom. wide allows varying thicknesses to be firmly held. A strip of glass-

Fig. 19

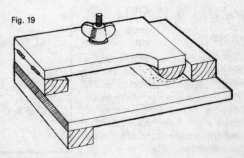

paper on the base further helps with the grip. The right-hand side of the clamp piece is cut away to give clearance to the finger holding the saw handle.

This sawing board has proved very popular with students who are in no way handicapped.

Fig. 20

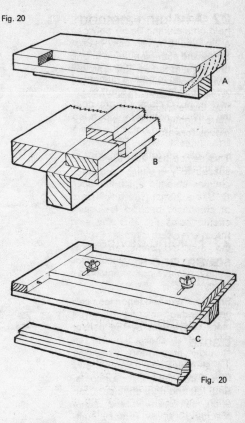

20 Sticking board

The sticking board, **A** and **B**, is the traditional way of holding narrow components for rebating, ploughing and planing or scratching mouldings. The board can be built up or rebated. A number of such boards will be needed in different sizes. **C** shows an adjustable sticking board which will meet the great majority of requirements. A small clipped off nail helps to hold the work firm on either board but on the finest work this may well have to be removed. The fence may be built up or the slots can be cut out of the solid.

Fig. 20

21 Panel fielding aid

The fielding of panels can be much simplified with this aid. Panels do not always cramp easily to the bench top. This model, if not made too small, will cover a range of panel sizes. It will not only hold the workpiece firmly but will also provide a fence against which a jack or rebate plane can run.

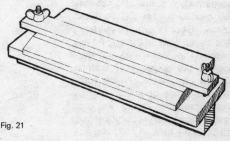

Fig. 21

22 A holding method

This method was found convenient for holding chair seats for hollowing and finishing and has since proved to have a number of other applications. A stout block permits two G clamps to grip near the sides. A notched support leg forced into place holds the whole arrangement firm. The workpiece can be rotated to work in any direction.

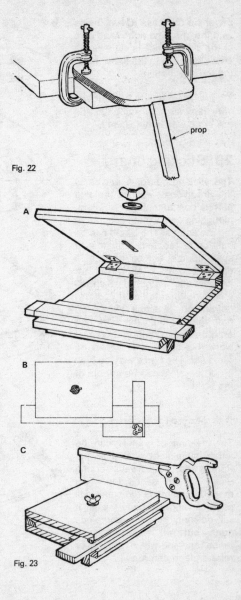

Fig. 22

prop

23 Holding device to square and saw shoulders

Small mortise and tenon jobs can be speeded up and rendered more convenient by the use of this aid. **B** shows squaring a shoulder preparatory to knifing the shoulder line and **C** shows how convenient the sawing is. Both left and right shoulders can often be sawn at the same cramping. **A** is virtually self-explanatory. Solid wood or blockboard may be used and the hinging strip, if 25mm (1in) thick will cope with most work. The stop bar should be thinner than any of the work anticipated. A half-round strip on the hinged member provides a firm pressure over a range of sizes. A 10mm (⅜in) screw and wing nut will give adequate cramping.

Fig. 23

24 Holding slightly-shaped work in the vice

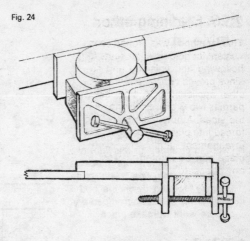

Fig. 24

When planing slightly-shaped work in the vice it is inevitable that it will see-saw. This can be prevented by supporting it on a packing piece, or pieces, of suitable thickness which rest on the vice bars.

25 Cleaning up a small table

All that is required here is a stout, nicely-planed board. The table is threaded round the vice and is held in place by this board. If the legs are tapered insert a small wedge under each. In this position the horns can be sawn off and the surface conveniently planed and sanded.

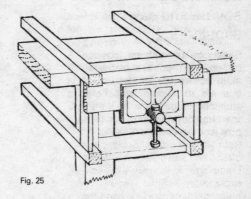

Fig. 25

26 Cleaning up a table top

Any large board can conveniently be held in this manner. Probably three-quarters of it can be comfortably worked from the far side of the bench. Prepare a stout block, slightly angled, and face one side with carpet. The work is cramped to this with two G cramps. When the block is gripped by the vice it will rotate slightly, forcing down the board very firmly at the uncramped end where work will take place.

27 Bridge cramping

An awkward-shaped workpiece on to which G cramps will not conveniently fit can often be held firm by the bridging techique. A block is produced of the same thickness as the job. A stout piece bridges the gap between the two. This can be held with a G cramp or by a strong bolt through a hole in the bench top.

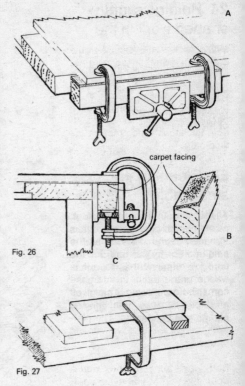

carpet facing

Fig. 26

Fig. 27

28 Picture frame cramps

Many commercial picture-frame cramps deal with only one corner at a time, thus requiring nails. A quality frame with a glued joint reinforced by veneer 'feathers' requires all the joints to be glued at the same time.

The simple type, **A**, can be produced as a rebated strip then sawn off to make four blocks. Chisel or file the notches.

The thread through type, **B**, is easier to use but is more complex to make. Saw and chisel out the small platform, then drill for the cord. A refinement is to drill a hole of about 5mm ($\frac{3}{16}$in) in the corner before sawing. This gives a little clearance right in the corner when gluing up. The platform should be kept well waxed in use.

Both types are tensioned with a double length of thin nylon cord. The four twisting sticks must always be rotated in the same way, for example clockwise. When cramped up check for equal diagonals to ensure frame is square. If not, two V-blocks of thin ply screwed to a flat board will correct this, **C**. Over correct, allowing for spring back.

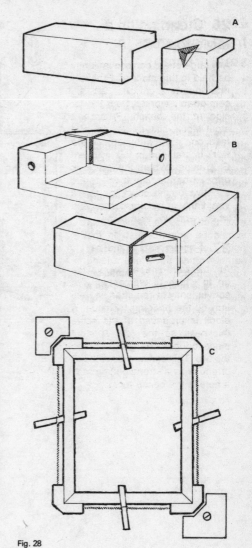

Fig. 28

29 Light picture framing cramps for small frames

Tensioning by twisted string is not practicable on very small frames. As very little pressure is required, however, rubber bands can be substituted. These corner blocks generally need to be quite thin and the grain direction can be either of those shown. Drill the corners out before sawing. This gives clearance for the sharp corner of the mitre, making sure that the pressure is where it should be and not just on the point. Fit screw hooks and assemble round the frame adding rubber bands until sufficient pressure is built up. Glue up on a sheet of thin polythene on a flat surface such as chipboard.

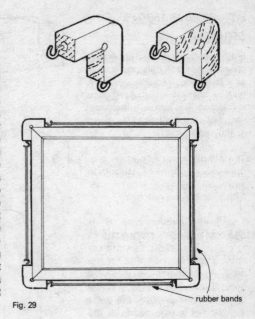

Fig. 29

rubber bands

30 Screw adjusted light cramps

The illustration shows this further alternative. The screw and wing nut should be about 4mm ($\frac{3}{16}$in). The three plain blocks should have their corners well rounded to permit the cord to move easily. A thin woven nylon cord is suitable. When tightening the wing nut it may be necessary just to grip the screwed rod with pliers to prevent rotation.

31 Mitre cramp and corrector

Mitres in small frames can be accurately made without a shooting board by the use of this aid. It consists of a blockboard or plywood base, under which is fixed a stout block for gripping in the bench vice. Two hardwood blocks with mitred corners are glued and screwed to the top, making an accurate right-angle. The top is protected by a piece of hardboard.

The joint, which has been cut on an ordinary mitre box, can be glued in a straightforward manner using two G cramps. If, however, the joint is not a good fit when cramped up dry, open the joint very slightly, then cramp again. Run a fine saw through the joint, blow out the sawdust and recramp.

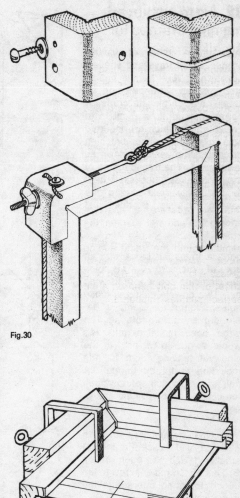

Fig.30

Fig. 31

use hardboard waste
piece to saw into

32 Jig to cut keyed mitres

The mitred joints of picture frames, small trays and shallow boxes 'are very fragile unless strengthened. Strengthening by small nails or pins is crude. A better method is a number of sawcuts into which are inserted small triangles of either matching or contrasting veneer, known as feathers, **A**. The fragile nature of the joint makes it necessary for it to be firmly held during the sawing. This jig, **B**, does just that.

The back plate of multi-ply supports a triangular block with an apex of exactly 90°, **C**. This holds the clamping screw with its wing nut. Two dowels, fitting in loose holes, support the clamping bar and prevent it from rotating. The large base block permits the whole device to be held in the vice yet leaving room for the moulding to thread through. A pair of simple coil springs open the clamp bar to facilitate operation.

Very small frames may not fit on this vice-held device. For them a smaller device has been drawn, **D**. This will cramp or screw to the bench top then operate in the same way.

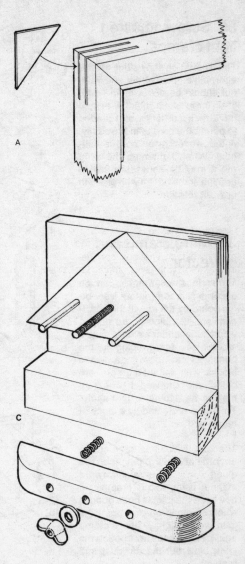

A

C

33 Saddle to hold boxes

Boxes with mitred or lapped joints can have their corners strengthened by means of veneer keys. This technique is particularly suited for boxes which are to be veneered, **A**. Larger boxes can be threaded over the front jaws of the vice. Smaller boxes present a holding problem. The mitred joints are very fragile during the sawing process.

This saddle type jig, **B**, can either be held in the vice or screwed to the bench top. The box can be firmly held with two small G cramps for the sawing.

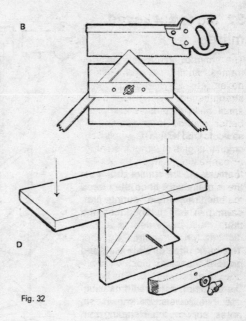

Fig. 32

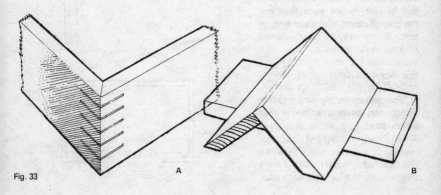

Fig. 33

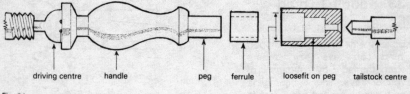

driving centre   handle   peg   ferrule   loosefit on peg   tailstock centre

loosefit on ferrule

Fig. 34

34 Pusher for ferrules

Ferrules, to be successful, must be a really tight fit on the turned handle. The ferrule is made first, from thin wall tubing, then the stub must be turned to a very tight fit. It now requires a pusher to put on the ferrule easily and square.

The pusher is turned from mild steel to the section shown. No sizes are important apart from the diameter and depth of the large ferrule hole. A small through hole is well countersunk to take the tail-stock centre. When pushing the ferrule on to the handle, make sure that the parting off point is not too thin. A sash cramp may be used instead of a lathe for pressure.

35 Box holder

A box, before its top or bottom is fitted, can be conveniently held by the device, **B**, in the vice as in **A**. The central member, approximately the same thickness as the box side, is planed to a very slight taper to give opening jaws.

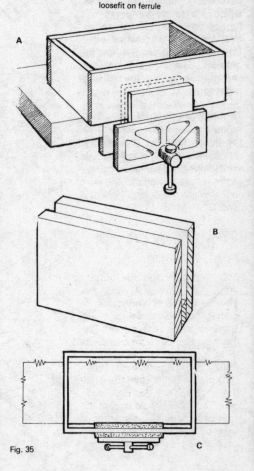

Fig. 35

This gives firm holding for working on the top edge, unimpeded by cramps, **C**. Where, however, a bottom has been fitted, a stout board held in the vice, and two G cramps is the best that can be done, **D**.

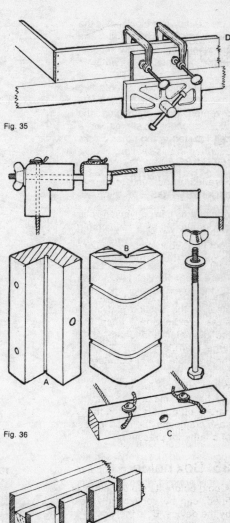

Fig. 35

36 Cramp for small mitred boxes

This is only a development of the picture frame cramp, Fig. 30. Four corner blocks are made to suit the sizes of box commonly made. Three are as **B**, one is as **A** and block **C** is the adjustable anchorage for the cord or wire. The cord holes in **C** match up with those in **A** and the grooves in **B**. Tension is achieved using a 4mm ($\frac{3}{16}$in) screwed rod and wing nut through the central hole in **A** and **C**.

37 Hanging rack for sash cramps

This method holds the cramps firmly and safely, **A**. It allows them to be stored very close together thus economising in wall space which is always short. The block can be cut from one piece or built up and, if built up, the front can be made from 13mm ($\frac{1}{2}$in) ply for extra strength. Illustration **B** makes the idea obvious. The slots should accept the cramp bar easily, the groove behind the front face should accept the foot of the screw end

Fig. 36

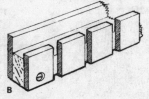

Fig. 37

of the cramp. The block holds the cramp very firmly by the feet and very safely. It is virtually impossible for the cramp to fall out.

The lower block, **C**, serves two purposes. Firstly the cramp bar is prevented from damaging the wall. Secondly it serves as a shelf for storing the other blocks described in this section.

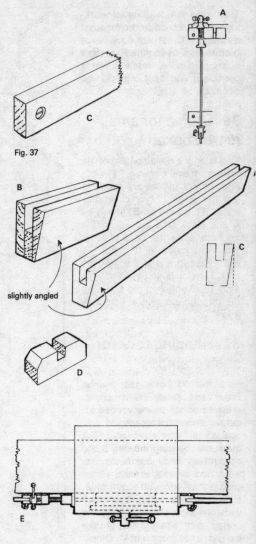

Fig. 37

38 Sash cramp accessories

Wide boards can conveniently be held for planing by a sash cramp gripped in the vice, where the inner wood jaw of the vice projects beyond the bench edge. Where the inner vice jaw is flush with the bench edge or where it is required to hold a piece smaller than the vice jaws an alternative method is necessary. Several grooved blocks of different lengths are needed. There is no point in making these longer than the vice jaws but one or two smaller ones are often useful. They can be either grooved, **A**, or built up, **B**. In either case the groove should be an easy fit on the cramp bar. One side of the block should be very slightly angled, **C**, so that the cramp bar is firmly gripped when the vice is tightened. The total width must exceed the size of the sash cramp foot. Height will depend on individual circumstances. The arrangement seen from above is shown at **E**.

Fig. 38

Sash cramps invariably topple over at the most inconvenient moment. A set of auxiliary wooden feet, preferably identical, is useful here, **D**. Use a hard hardwood, suitable sizes are about 100 × 40 × 22mm (4 × 1½ × ⅞in).

39 Aids to large door fitting

The edges of large doors are usually planed by standing astride the door and gripping with the knees, a thoroughly inconvenient position. The method shown in **A** is a considerable improvement. The cost is negligible and the device is easily transported. It consists of one or, preferably, two stout blocks of about 100 × 75mm (4 × 3in). A central slot is cut wide enough for the thickest door likely to be encountered. A tapered socket is cut to a depth of about 25mm (1in). A wedge is made to suit this. Well-fitting wedges, tightly driven home, produce a very rigid structure on which it is very easy and comfortable to plane.

The rocker shaped foot lift, **B**, is a great help to anyone hinging a heavy door without assistance. A suitable material is 50 × 50mm (2 × 2in) hardwood. Quite thin ends are required with a smooth curve to the centre. The method of use is obvious, as shown in **C**. Other applications will be found.

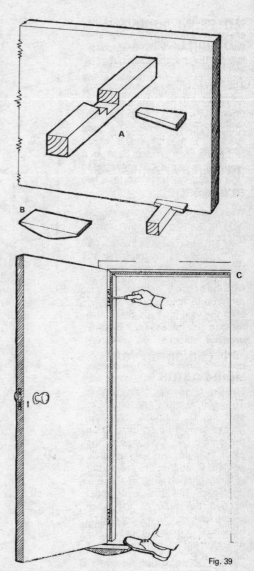

Fig. 39

40 Right-angled holding brackets

The better form of bracket is made from two hardwood strips dovetailed and glued together. A plywood fillet preserves the right-angle exactly, **A**. A simpler and quicker, though not such a good version, is also shown, **B**, made from one solid piece of hardwood with holes bored and enlarged to the shape illustrated to take two G cramps.

Illustration **C** shows a dovetail joint being firmly held for marking. On wide carcase joints a pair of brackets is an improvement. The brackets are also useful for assembling simpler, nailed and glued butt joints and lapped joints and for holding dowelled joints during the drilling.

41 Gluing-up very thin boards

Thin boards, when cramped together with a number of sash cramps, invariably buckle. This method, commonly used by guitar makers is both simple and successful. Having planed the joint, usually on a shooting board, it is laid on a piece of blockboard, with a thin lath 20 × 6mm ($\frac{3}{4}$ × $\frac{1}{4}$in) underneath the joint. Two thin hardwood strips are pressed firmly against the edges and are screwed there as in **A**; the lath is then removed. **B**

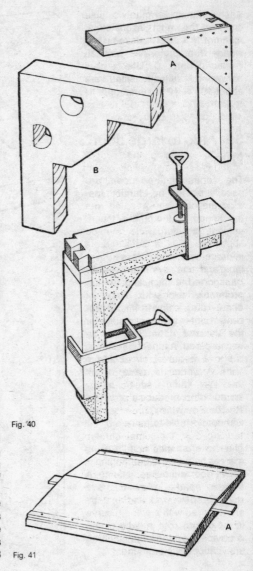

Fig. 40

Fig. 41

shows the actual glue up. Glue the joint then return to the blockboard with a strip of waxed paper below and above the joint. By means of a stout batten slightly curved in length and two cramps the two boards are sprung together. This method makes sure of a good cramp up and a flat board.

When uncramping after twenty-four hours, first release one of the screwed strips. This will prevent the jointed board from springing up.

42 Violin cramps

A large number of these lightweight cramps are needed when gluing on the back and front of stringed instruments. They are cheap and easy to make and have numerous applications in the workshop. The diagrams are self-explanatory. Some round stock is prepared, by turning or with a rounder, to 38mm (1⅜in) diameter. On the sawbench cut up the blocks, then suitably drill for the 5mm (¼in) threaded rod. Some of the blocks need the tapping drill, the remainder are given a clearance hole. Secure the rod in the threaded hole with an epoxy resin glue. Glued on leather pads prevent both damage to the work and rotation.

The lighter model, **A**, adjusts with a wing nut and the handled version, **B**, is an improvement.

Fig. 41

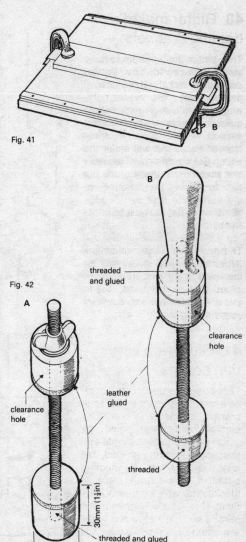

Fig. 42

threaded and glued

clearance hole

leather glued

threaded

clearance hole

A

B

30mm (1¼in)

threaded and glued

38mm (1⅜in)

43 Guitar maker's cramp

Fig. 43

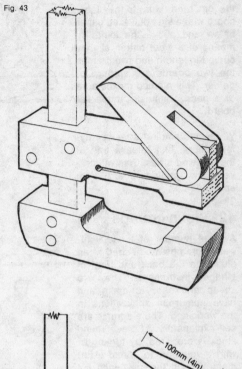

This cam cramp appears to have been developed by guitar makers to satisfy their special needs. They had to be light-weight, have a long reach and, as quite a number were required, cheap. Beech or any close-grained hardwood will make the jaws. Cramp the two together and bore out the ends of the cut out. In sawing the tenon make the spring cut first then wedge this open to get the best possible sawcut.

The bar is from light aluminium alloy. In the moving bar drill for the pins very accurately. To avoid work on the joints, it is in fact possible to build up the jaws from three layers.

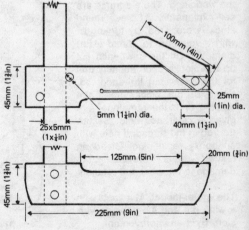

45mm (1¾in)

25x5mm (1x¼in)

5mm (1½in) dia.

100mm (4in)

25mm (1in) dia.

40mm (1½in)

45mm (1¾in)

125mm (5in)

20mm (¾in)

225mm (9in)

MARKING
AIDS

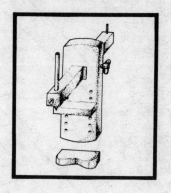

44 Straight-edge

A straight-edge, longer than the normal steel versions of 500mm–1m (2–3ft), is occasionally required. Select the wood carefully using only well-seasoned stable hardwood. Produce to size, then true up the true edge ideally by machine planing. The other edge should be slightly shaped to avoid confusion. Drill a hanging hole and always hang when not in use, leaning against a wall over a period will bow the straight-edge. Varnish or paint well as this not only helps to reduce movement, but by making it readily identifiable as a tool also prevents misuse in a communal workshop.

45 Diagonal laths

A pair of laths, **A**, will check the equality of diagonals inside a frame or carcase. Push firmly into two corners and make the pencil mark shown. Repeat in the other corners and compare. Using this method and measuring the combined sticks enables a length to be measured in a place where a rule cannot be held, e.g. from the bottom of one small hole to the bottom of another.

Model **B** is more commonly used where cramps and other restrictions are not in the way. Make the two pencil marks and adjust the cramps to give the mean reading.

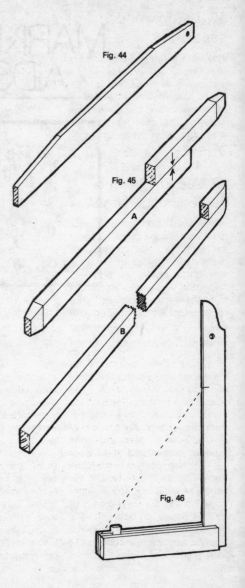

Fig. 44

Fig. 45

A

B

Fig. 46

46 Large wooden square

This is used not so much for checking right-angles, the diagonal lath is more accurate, but for marking out large components of plywood and other sheet material. It should not be used with the marking knife which damages it.

47 Aid for copying angles in buildings

When building in fitments to a room one is soon made aware of the fact that few corners are really right-angles. In order to saw large pieces of plywood, chipboard and similar materials to fit the corner exactly a large copying square is needed and 750 × 600mm (30 × 24in) is a useful size.

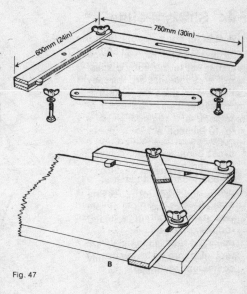

Fig. 47

This can best be made by laminating strips of hardwood or plywood as shown in **A**. The stock is of three layers, the centre one stopped well short of the rounded end. The blade is of a single layer also with one rounded end. Cut a short 6mm ($\frac{1}{4}$in) slot in the centre of the blade and drill a 6mm ($\frac{1}{4}$in) hole in the centre of the stock and a same-sized hole in the curved ends of both. A 6mm ($\frac{1}{4}$in) bolt with wing nut makes the pivot. A diagonal brace is necessary in order not to lose the angle during handling and this is made of the same material again with the ends drilled and rounded. A small stud inserted into the centre layer prevents the square from tilting in use.

Push the device hard into the corner to be measured and preserve the angle by fastening the brace. This must be fixed to the side convenient for the subsequent marking on the board. Illustration **B** shows how the angle is transferred to the board.

48 Try-square pencil gauge

This is a useful tool for rough marking out in the early stages. Many try squares are already calibrated, making the work that much easier. Drill holes at convenient intervals, 10mm or ½in, of a size to accept either a pencil point or a ballpoint pen.

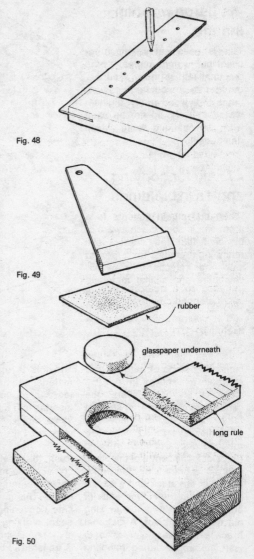

Fig. 48

49 Glue up square

This useful tool for checking angles when gluing up is simply made from truly flat plywood grooved into a wood stock. It is very robust and should stay accurate. Be sure to wash off any glue it picks up immediately.

Fig. 49

50 Setting out square and gauge

This is useful for setting out full-size designs or full-size details of larger work. The stock can be chopped from the solid or, more accurately, built up. It should be a tight working fit on a metre (3ft) rigid rule. A hole of about 25mm (1in) is bored in the top side and a well-fitting plug is turned to fit it. One surface is faced with fine glasspaper. With the rule in place the plug is dropped in, glasspaper down, and a square of thin rubber is glued over the top. This tool can be used either as a T square or, locked by pressure on the rubber, as a pencil gauge.

rubber

glasspaper underneath

long rule

Fig. 50

51 Four-way block gauge

Made from small pieces of very hard hardwood several of these small block gauges prove very handy. Four rebates can be cut each increasing in size by 1mm ($\frac{1}{16}$in). They are used with pencil or ballpoint pen for rough marking out or in situations where the conventional marking gauge is unsuitable.

52 The double chamfer gauge

This is similar in style to the block gauge. Rebates are cut with an allowance for pencil thickness. The corners are rounded to a quarter circle to mark stopped chamfers.

53 Depth gauge

This can be made in various sizes and fitted with a dowel, pencil or ballpoint pen. Alternative clampings are shown in **A**, **B** and **C**. The larger sizes are handy to gauge the depth when turning bowls. Small versions fitted with a ballpoint pen or pencil are useful with a router. In making housings, as at **D** overleaf, the cut is continually increased until the gauge will no longer mark.

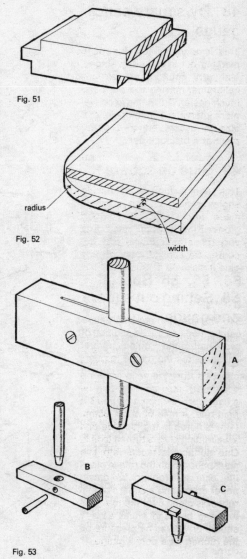

Fig. 51

Fig. 52

radius

width

Fig. 53

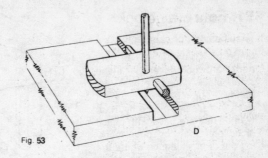

Fig. 53

D

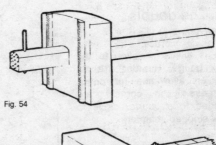

Fig. 54

54, 55, 56 Special gauges

54. The common marking gauge can be modified by the addition of two half-round guide strips. These permit the gauge to operate successfully on curved edges.

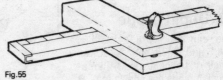

Fig.55

55. A rule gauge for pencil work. The sliding block can either be cut out or built up. This device is particularly useful for marking out wide sheet material.

56. A small steel cutter shaped to fit the end of a normal marking gauge and screwed into place permits marking in otherwise inaccessible places such as corners.

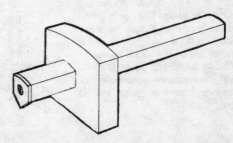

Fig.56

57 Panel gauge

It is customary for panel gauges to run on a rebate as it is not the practice to roll the gauge over, as is the method with the marking gauge. Three possible stem ends are shown. When using a gauge point, **A**, the end is thickened with a section of wood to match up with the rebate. If a pencil is used this is not necessary. The pencil may be held with a machine screw, **B**, or a wooden wedge, **C**. In the latter case it is convenient to slot the end on the circular saw and fill in to make the sloping mortise. The stem can be locked either with a wedge, **D**, or a screw, **E**. If the screw is chosen it must grip on a brass shoe as shown.

58 Pencil gauge for curved work

This is similar to Fig. 57 except that the rebate is replaced by two dowels. Suitable sizes are approximate. Stock – 105 × 75 × 21mm (4 × 3 × ⅞in). Stem – 18–20mm (⅝–¾in) square.

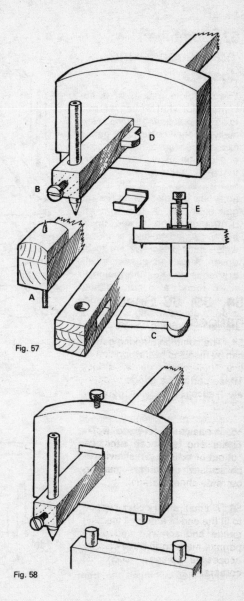

Fig. 57

Fig. 58

59 Combined 'grasshopper' and deep gauge

Fig. 59

The complete gauge, **A**, is assembled for what is often referred to as 'grasshopper gauging'. Normally a pencil or ballpoint pen is fixed in the stem although a point end can be used. The auxiliary fence is secured with round-headed screws through a suitable pair of holes. **B** shows the gauge in use. A box with an, overhanging top tacked on is being gauged to give a line on which nails or screws are to be driven. A second, curved, auxiliary fence enables the gauge to work round a curve. Without either fence the gauge becomes a deep gauge. Using a pencil or ballpoint, gauging can be carried out over a step or lipping, **C**, or down into a cavity.

60 Gauge with additional pencil end

The stem of an ordinary marking gauge has been reversed, **A**. The other end, as in **B**, has been bored, filed up as shown and fitted with a small machine screw.

61 Gauging set-in shelves

Frequently it is required to gauge the mortises and tenons on shelves set in behind the front

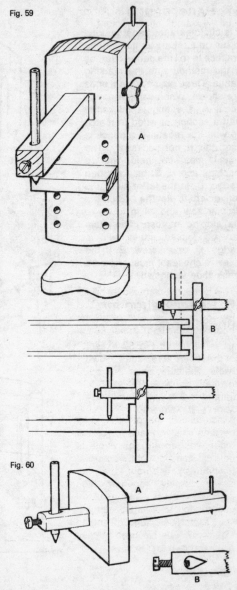

Fig. 60

edge of the carcase side. A typical jointing arrangement is shown with the customary housing omitted for simplicity.

Fig. 61

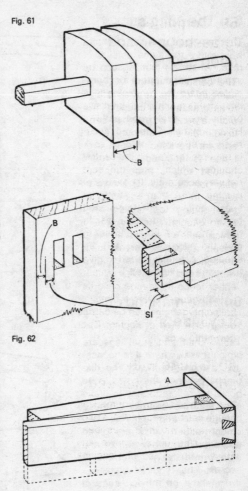

Decide the amount of set in and prepare a block that thickness as at B. Any accurately thicknessed hardwood will do but multiply is excellent. In use the block is slid onto the stem and the combined gauge is set for the shelf tenon. Afterwards the block is removed and, without adjustment the mortises in the carcase side marked. If well made these blocks are worth keeping to be used for the setting of rails for table or stool construction, etc.

62 Gauging tapers

This is a convenient aid for gauging such items as legs tapered on the inside. It consists of a long hardwood member about 20mm ($\frac{3}{4}$in) thick on to which is dovetailed a short member of the same material, **A**. If the long member is made wider, as indicated by the dotted lines, the whole can be easily held in the bench vice for gauging. A small packing block is made to suit the taper required and the whole is held by hand or lightly cramped for gauging. The right taper can be accurately repeated any number of times. A particularly useful application is the gauging with a mortise gauge of angled tenons such as are used in chair making shown in plan at **B**.

Fig. 62

63 The pitch stick

The back legs of a set of chairs will require the same amount of rake. While the first leg can be accurately set out from a square-edged board the remaining legs nest inside each other and are drawn from a plywood pattern. Having planed these as accurately as possible, the pitch stick is required for planing the central shoulder which takes the seat rail very accurately. It consists of nothing more than a length of seasoned, accurately-planed hardwood and a dowel in a tight hole. The dowel is tapped out to give the pitch required and the shoulder carefully planed to give the result as illustrated.

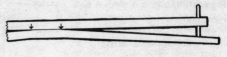

Fig. 63

64 The marking out of cylinders

Table, chair and stool legs are typical cases where it is necessary to mark identically the distances between the holes to be bored for rails and also to make sure that the centres of these holes are in a straight line. Two straight-edged strips are glued and pinned together with an end stop forming a type of cradle, **A** and **B**. The required distances are marked on the top edge of the cradle measured from the end stop. Ruling along the top edge easily produces centres accurately in line, **C**. Strong rubber bands are adequate to hold the component still while marking.

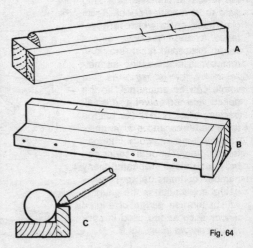

Fig. 64

65 Curved components

Curved components present a holding problem when marking out using the jig described in Fig. 64. The easiest solution is to make an identical pair of wooden collars which will fit on each end of the component and in this form it can be conveniently held in the jig.

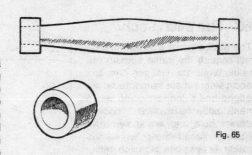

Fig. 65

66 Gauging cylinders

Cylinders require gauging in length to mark a straight centre line for drilling or for marking in-line mortises. Chair, table and stool legs are cases in point.

First a cradle is made and this is most easily constructed from two sections glued together with a base block which permits the cradle to be held in the vice. The work can be firmly held by a suitably placed G cramp, gripping on a shaped block as indicated by the dotted line in the diagram. A special gauge is required with an unusually deep stock. A tapered dowel wedge is quite adequate to lock the stem. Suitable stems can be arranged to take one point, two points for mortise gauging, or a ballpoint pen. In use make sure that there is good contact between the stock and the cradle.

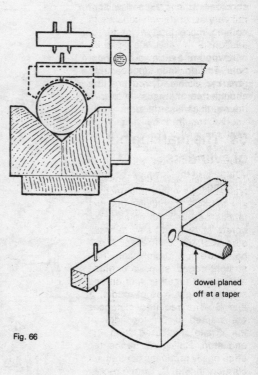

dowel planed off at a taper

Fig. 66

67 Matching curves

Lines can easily by drawn to copy curves, **A**, by turning up several suitable discs from thin plywood, acrylic or plastic laminate. In the lathe drill a central hole to take a fine ballpoint pen, **B**. The two methods of use are shown at **C**. On the right the disc works outside a template. On the left it works inside either a template or a bent lath. **P** is the pen position.

68 Marking curves

Curves are best marked along a curved lath lined up over three marked points. There are three suggested methods. A lath of even thickness is bent to the curve required by nipping the ends in a sash cramp, **A**. A well-chosen lath of even thickness, bent by a twisted string in the manner of the bowsaw, **B**. Finally the most rigid and reliable of the three, a small pointed block, **D**, positions the lath at its centre, **C**. The two ends are pulled back to the marks and cramped there.

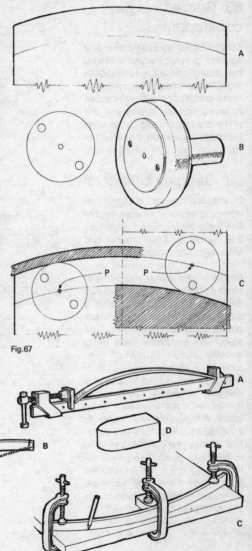

Fig.67

Fig. 68

69 Alternative gauge construction

Most of the gauges described already can also be made by this method. It has the advantage that no mortising is required. Using a ballpoint pen means that it is not necessary to roll the gauge on to its corner as with the normal marking gauge. The step, therefore, is quite a convenience.

First prepare stem material of about 20 × 20mm ($\frac{3}{4}$ × $\frac{3}{4}$in), sufficient for a long and a short stem with some extra. Two small offcuts with well-squared ends can be glued between two wider blocks to make the stock. A well waxed offcut can be used as a spacer to give a true square hole. More of the same material can thicken up the stem to carry a normal ballpoint pen. This stem and likewise the stock are drilled and slotted with a fairly wide sawcut.

The clamping screw can be made by threading or soldering a 5mm ($\frac{1}{4}$in) wing nut to a No. 12 brass woodscrew. A normal woodscrew will suit in the stem. Drill the correct clearance and pilot holes. In a good hardwood these threads will last a very long time. A plain stem may be exactly drilled to take a ballpoint refill. Cut the rebate and shape the ends. A shaving may be needed from the stems to give a working fit in the stock.

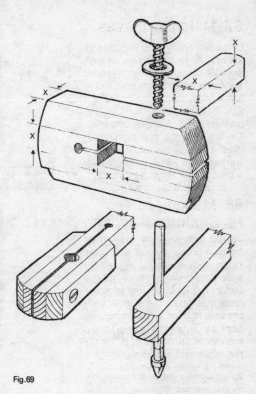

Fig. 69

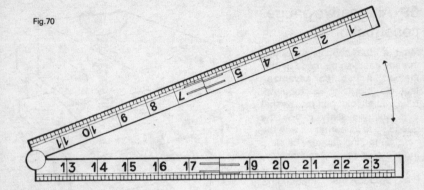

Fig.70

70 Setting out angles

The folding two feet rule enables the setting out of commonly used angles with considerable accuracy. Simply look up the distance in the table and set up the rule as in the table.

Angle	Distance	Angle	Distance
10°	$2\frac{1}{8}$in	40°	$8\frac{3}{16}$in
15°	$3\frac{3}{16}$in	45°	$9\frac{1}{8}$in
20°	$4\frac{3}{16}$in	50°	$10\frac{1}{8}$in
22$\frac{1}{2}$°	$4\frac{11}{16}$in	60°	12 in
25°	$5\frac{3}{16}$in	67$\frac{1}{2}$°	$13\frac{5}{16}$in
30°	$6\frac{1}{4}$in	90°	17in

71 Marking identical angles

When angles other than 90° are to be marked a sliding bevel is usually set. Apart from the difficulty of setting really accurately, a drop or a knock will lose the angle and resetting later in the job is difficult. An altogether more satisfactory method is to make a tapered block to suit the angle and interpose this between the job and the square. In this way the angle can be accurately repeated as often as necessary.

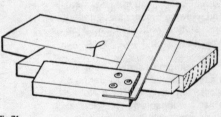

Fig.71

Since metrication a more comprehensive table of angles has been prepared using the four fold 1 metre rule. This has been added on page 215.

72 Scribers for levelling table legs

However carefully a table or chair is glued up, when placed on a level surface there is invariably some wobble. A scriber can be used to ensure equal lengths and two types are shown. The rectangular one, **A**, has a marking gauge point at each end. By careful positioning of the points at different distances from the four faces eight different scribing heights are possible. The circular model, **B**, takes more making but gives an infinite number of scribing heights.

To use, stand on a truly flat surface such as the circular saw table and level up the table or chair with a wedge under each foot, making sure with a long rule that the top rail is at an equal height at each corner. Now scribe a line on four sides of each leg leaving the smallest amount which can conveniently be sawn off.

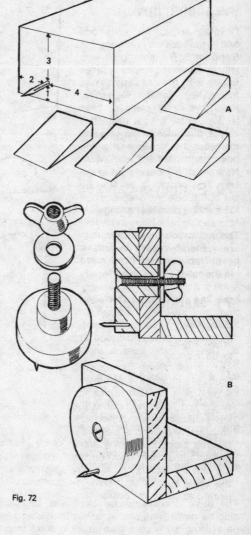

Fig. 72

73 Dovetails – setting the sliding bevel

Dovetail angles for softwoods and hardwoods vary between 1 in 6 and 1 in 8. The most convenient way to set sliding bevels to these angles is by the use of a dovetail board kept in the workshop. Paint a suitable piece of 9mm (⅜in) plywood a light distinctive colour, drill holes for hanging and mark out the slopes with a fine point permanent felt marker, **A**. Note the 1 in 7 bevel right at the end. This permits a bevel to be set at the nearly closed position for marking dovetail halvings.

The angles of dovetail halvings are generally marked with a bevel from the end. This is not ideal since the bearing surface is always small and often not very true. The marking is better done from the edge using the bevel set as described, or better still using the special marker illustrated at **B**. This is made from a short length of hardwood with a slot into which is glued a piece of plastic laminate. When dry, plane or file to the required angle – usually 1 in 7. If, when using this tool, the angle is marked to a short distance from the corner, **C**, the waste can be sawn off thus obviating the less accurate and slower paring from a corner.

The basic dovetail marker can also be made from plastic laminate using an impact glue and pins, **D**. This gives a thinner tool than a wooden one and is easier to make than a metal one.

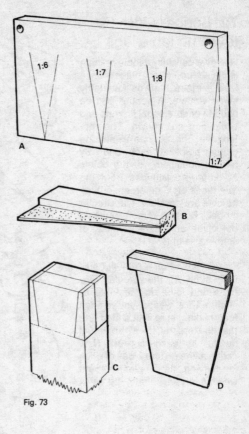

Fig. 73

74 Dovetail marking system

There are many types of dovetail marker and as many methods of using them, but I like to think that this marker, **A**, and its method is pre-eminent.

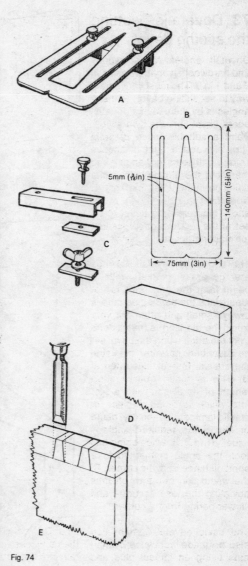

The plate is made from a piece of 20 gauge brass, steel or alloy 140 × 75mm (5½ × 3in). This should be sawn and not cut with snips as these may permanently distort it. Drill the four 5mm ($\frac{3}{16}$in) and three 1mm ($\frac{3}{32}$in) corner holes, then sufficient smaller holes to get in a hacksaw blade to cut out the dovetail angle and the two slots. File to shape with great care, rounding the external corners and softening the edges. From an accurate centre line, file the two nicks as shown in **B**. The bar is a piece of brass channel 10 × 10 × 1.5mm ($\frac{3}{8}$ × $\frac{3}{8}$ × $\frac{1}{16}$in) and it has one threaded hole and a slot. The hole is threaded 2BA. A sliding block is fitted below the slot and this, too, is threaded 2BA. The bar is secured to the plate, preferably with a pair of 2BA electrical terminals or with wing nuts and washers, **C**.

Prepare the components and gauge to thickness on the piece which is to contain the tails, **D**. Choose a suitable bevel-edged chisel which is only slightly smaller than the chosen size of pin, **E**. Place the gauge on the work and adjust the bar to give a

Fig. 74

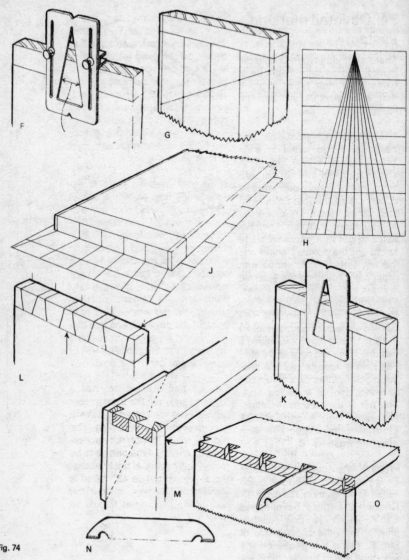

Fig. 74

width on the gauge line only slightly more than the chisel size, **F**. True up the bar with the edge of the gauge, either by a try square or against the edge of the wood. For angled dovetails use a sliding bevel on the angle already on the wood.

The two outside or half pins must be a little larger than half size, so, with a pencil, gauge mark down the two outside centre lines to achieve this effect. About 3mm ($\frac{1}{8}$in) is usual for medium-sized dovetails. The distance between these two lines is divided equally in the standard way to give the centre lines of all the pins, **G**. Alternatively a rapid calculator can be made to fix centre lines by drawing equi-spaced converging lines on a piece of plywood as in **H**. The horizontal lines are parallel, and the end of the piece of wood is offered up to the required number of converging lines and kept parallel to the horizontals. The centre lines are then easily picked off, **J**.

The gauge is now placed on the wood with the nick over each centre line in turn for the pins to be marked, ideally with a fine ballpoint pen, **K**. Shellac brushed on gives the surface a 'bite' on which to mark. On the end grain the square marking is done with a marking awl which provides a small groove into which the chisel can be put decisively should there be any error in sawing. Beginners can run a thick pencil into it. Two pencil lines will be formed, and one line should be removed with the saw, **L**. The two pieces are held together for the marking of the second piece, **O**. A pair of holding brackets, **M**, is useful for this process see Fig. 40; one will do for small work. The two pieces are held to the bracket with light G cramps.

A dovetail marking knife is essential for fine dovetails but is useful for all sizes, **N**. It is made from a piece of tool steel 100–125mm (4–5in) long by 12 × 1·5mm ($\frac{1}{2} \times \frac{1}{16}$in) and a piece from a power hacksaw blade is very suitable. Both the little bevels are on the same side, giving a left-hand and a right-hand knife. In use, **O**, the flat side is held hard against the dovetail, and this tool will get into the most inaccessible corner where the marking awl or pencil never got in the past.

The holding bracket, **M**, has a further use when the front or rear corner is to be mitred to take a groove, rebate or moulding. The mitre is often, though not necessarily, at 45° but if the pieces to be joined are not equal thicknesses, the angle cannot be 45°. What is important, however, is that the sum of the two angles should be 90°.

The remaining six diagrams, **P–U**, show how, when the pieces are held at 90°, both angles can be marked from the same edge, using a sliding bevel.

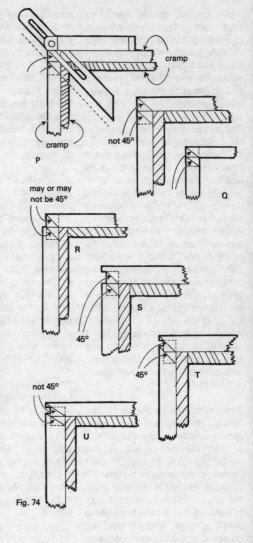

75 A dowel joint marker

This is an extremely useful aid for marking out dowelled joints, particularly in flat frames and tables. A piece of plastic laminate is sandwiched in a hardwood stock, **A**. The slot in the hardwood can be cut with a very thin circular saw or a sandwich is built up by gripping the blade in an engineer's vice, holding the wood blocks firmly down on the jaws while gluing. The glue joint is later strengthened by screwing, **B**. Mark one end of the stock black for easy reference.

To use, hold the tool on to the workpiece and draw round the latter. Draw the centre line and mark the dowel positions, **C**. In some cases it will be preferred to stagger the holes on each side of

Fig. 74

the centre line, **G**. Drill small holes to suit the available marking awl. Note whether the marking began at the black or white end and then line up this chosen end with the edge of the workpiece and prick through, **C**. Reposition on the other half of the joint and repeat, marking out the complete joint as in **E**. The opposite end of a frame is marked out by turning over the marker.

When insetting the rail on a stool or table as in **F**, simply insert a wood block of the thickness of the set-in when marking out for drilling, **D**. The marker can be used many times before it has too many holes drilled in it. After the first use, mark subsequent drillings by ringing with a felt-tipped pen, wiping off when the job is complete.

76 Holder to mark out table legs

Apart from freeing sash cramps this is a convenient device, particularly so in a communal workshop or when numbers of similar tables are being made. Any man-made board will serve for the base with the usual vice strip underneath. A permanent lip is glued on one edge. This must be considerably less than the thickness of the legs, in order that the square can operate conveniently. Two pairs of wedges complete the job, and hold the work firmly while the marking is carried out.

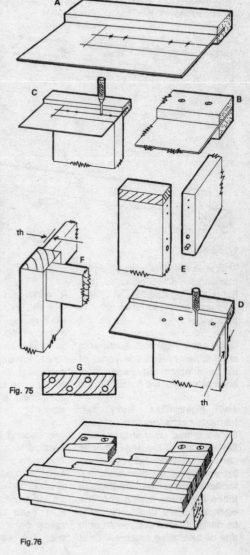

Fig. 75

Fig. 76

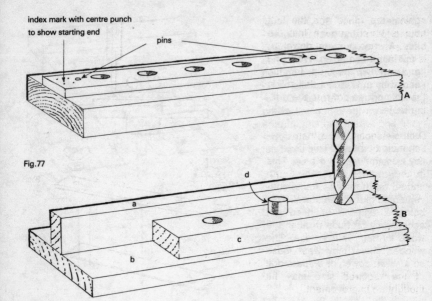

index mark with centre punch to show starting end

pins

Fig.77

a

d

b

c

A

B

77 Drilling a line of holes

Bookcases and cupboards with adjustable shelves are some of the jobs which require identical lines of equidistant holes.

The illustrations show two methods of achieving this. **A** shows a mild steel strip of, say, 20 × 3mm (¾ × ⅛in). This is carefully marked out with dividers and drilled. At intervals smaller holes are drilled and through these the guide is pinned to the workpiece. The drilling can now be done by hand drill, by electric drill or by drilling machine. Bear in mind that after a number of jobs the mild steel will wear and the holes will become sloppy. Do not enter the drill when revolving as this rapidly increases the wear. Identify one end of the guide with a file or punch mark so that the same end is always positioned at the start of the work.

The second method, **B**, is only suitable for the drilling machine. The base b, which may be solid wood or blockboard, is planed to take the width of the component in hand. A hardwood fence, **a**, is fixed to the base leaving space behind it for cramps to grip. The workpiece, **c**, is held against the fence and the first hole is bored through into the base. A wood or metal dowel, **d**, is put into these holes. Work and jig are now lined up for the second hole. With the drill still in the hole cramp down to the drilling table.

Drill the second hole then position it on the dowel. This lines up the work for the third hole. This in its turn lines up for the fourth and so on. It may be found convenient to glue in the dowel. This being a tight fit, it need not necessarily protrude through the work. After much use the wooden dowel may wear loose so a metal dowel, or a spare drill of the required size may be thought an improvement.

78 Veneer strip cutter for chess board

The base board of plywood or blockboard has a strip screwed to it for gripping in the vice and two machine screws are fitted at a centre distance of 430mm (17in) as at **E**. A hardboard strip, **D**, is drilled to fit over the machine screws. It is about 75mm (3in) wide. The veneer strip, **C**, has been cut to length to fit in between the screws. The steel cutting guide, **B**, 50mm (2in) wide, forms the top layer. It should first be gripped in a sash cramp which is tightened to bring on a bow which will give a good grip at the centre of the strip. The

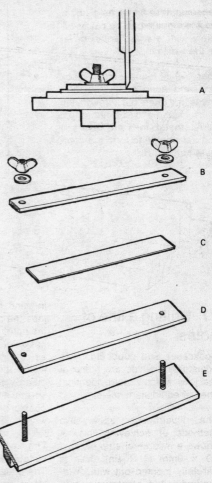

Fig. 78

veneer strips, firmly held under the steel guide can be cut accurately with a sharp knife, bevel on the waste side, **A**.

Four white and four black strips are taped together as in **F**. These are then put through the device again and cut into strips, **G**. Alternate strips are reversed and assembled to form the complete pattern, **H**.

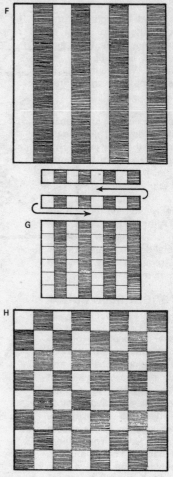

Fig. 78

TOOLS

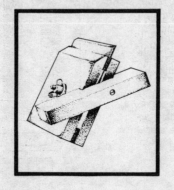

79 Oil pad

'Park your plane on its side lad'. This is a folk custom dating back to the age of wooden planes. The blades of these planes, were firmly held by a tightly hammered in wooden wedge. Following this advice however will disturb the lateral setting of an iron plane whose blade is nothing like so firmly held. Instead park the plane on the oil pad made by gluing a strip of carpet to a plane-sized board. This is a tidy arrangement which both protects the blade and reduces friction. Very little oil is needed.

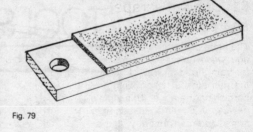

Fig. 79

80 Winding strips

This is probably the most essential of all the tools which cannot be bought and **A** shows one of a variety of patterns. Two identical strips are produced, exactly parallel, from well-seasoned, stable hardwood. They are tapered in section to produce a stable base. The rear strip remains light coloured. Two identical dark blocks are glued on or painted on at the corners. The whole of the front face is painted, stained or veneered to match the corner blocks. So is the top edge.

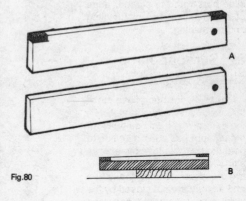

Fig.80

Winding strips are in fact magnifiers of twist or wind. They are placed on what is hoped will be a true face and viewed from a low viewpoint as in **B**. Any twist is shown as a white line at one side between two blacks.

Other design variations can be achieved by the use of inlay stringings. Suggested sizes would be 400–450mm × 50mm × 15mm (16–18in × 2in × ⅝in).

81 Cabinet scraper sharpening aid

The state of the jaws of the average woodworker's vice make it far from the ideal way of holding the thin scraper when filing and burnishing the edge. This simple device, **A**, holds the scraper firmly and conveniently and in addition eliminates the very unpleasant filing noise. It can be seen from the section, **B**, that there are two hardwood blocks with leather jaws which are kept apart by a thin and very slightly tapered slip glued between them. The height should be such that the device will rest on the vice slide bars with the scraper edge at a convenient height for filing and burnishing.

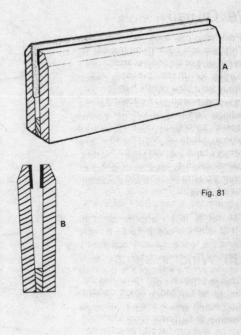

Fig. 81

82 Scraper plane sharpening aid

As these blades need filing not at 90°, as the scraper, but at 45°, the device which was suitable for the scraper has been modified to hold the blade at this angle while still filing horizontally. The jaws are narrower to suit the blade and as they are not closed by the vice, a tightening bolt and wing nut are fitted. A short bar is secured to one jaw (not both) at 45°. With this bar resting on the top of the vice, the blade is held at 45° for horizontal filing.

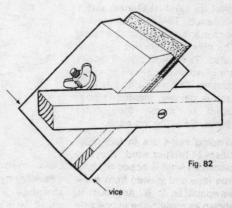

Fig. 82

vice

83 Scratch tools

The type of scratch tool most commonly used is illustrated at **A**. The block is quite straightforward being in two parts, each about 13mm (½in) thick and screwed together. Cutters can be made from pieces of power hacksaw blades, old handsaws or cabinet scrapers. They are filed to the shape of the moulding or groove required at an angle of 90° so as to be able to cut in both directions.

Model **B** is an improvement in that it has a comfortable handle and the fence is easily adjustable rather than the cutter. Model **C** works on the lines of the marking gauge. Its fence, however, is much wider which gives greater accuracy when cutting at some distance from the edge.

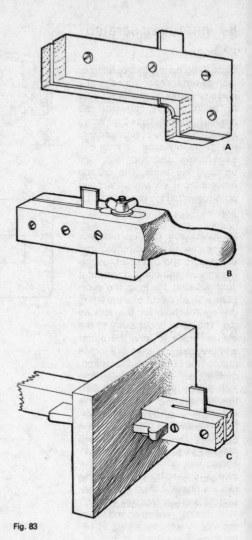

Fig. 83

84 Improved scratch tool

Scratching an ovolo moulding or a small rebate near the edge of a piece presents no problem since, if the tool slips outwards, no damage is caused. When scratching an inlay, for example, the same distance in from the edge, any outward slip will damage the work. The second fence will prevent this on all components within the capacity of the tool.

Mark out and cut the mortises before sawing off the fences and shaping. Prepare the stem slightly oversize and plane down for a tight working fit. Plug the mortises with an offcut of stem when drilling the hole for the locking pin. The stem is cut away at the centre, firstly to take the cutter and secondly to take the brass plate. This latter is cut to shape, drilled for the screws, then rounded on its lower edge. Cutters for this tool should be of a standard width and thickness. Ideal material is a heavy gauge cabinet scraper from which pieces can be sawn and filed.

For work on a corner or well in from an edge, one of the two fences is simply removed.

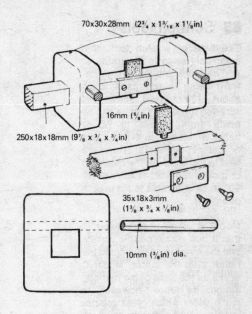

70×30×28mm (2¾ × 1³⁄₁₆ × 1⅛in)

16mm (⅝in)

250×18×18mm (9⅞ × ¾ × ¾in)

35×18×3mm
(1³⁄₈ × ¾ × ⅛in)

10mm (³⁄₈in) dia.

Fig. 84

85 Cutter for inlay grooves

Straight line grooves for inlay stringings are normally fairly near an edge, so can be cut with a two-knife cutting gauge. The stock for this, preferably with a step, can be of any of the forms previously described. That shown at **A** is slotted and tightened with a thumb screw. It may be mortised or built up.

The stem **B** must be a good working fit in the stock. The end is mortised to take the two cutting gauge knives and their spacing material. An ideal material is printers' type spacing, easily obtained from a jobbing printer since so little is required. Convenient sizes are 12 point or 14 point. 12 point is ($\frac{1}{6}$in) wide, 14 point is a little larger. A piece of square section type, **C**, is called an em space. Half of that is called an en and below this are thick, middle and thin spaces. Combining a small handful of these will give micrometer adjustment between the knives. If type is not obtainable wooden blocks and veneer shims will have to do.

86 Circular groove cutter

For cutting circular grooves a similar stem or arm is required as shown, the mortised end is thickened up before the mortise is

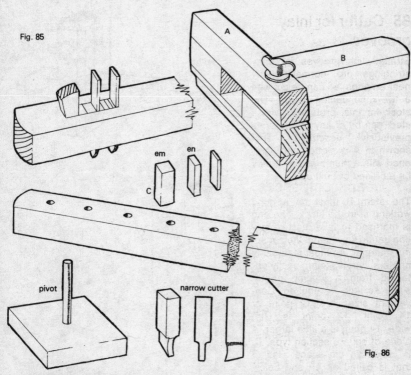

Fig. 85

em en

C

pivot

narrow cutter

Fig. 86

chopped. This should not be too short. From behind the mortise a series of holes is drilled. The spacing must be less than the mortise length. The pivot is made by fitting a long brass woodscrew to a wood block. Size is not vital – 8 or 10 gauge would suit but the holes in the stem must suit the screw. The head is countersunk on the underside and the thread sawn off leaving only the plain shank. The pivot block is glued to the work, with a paper joint

and using animal glues which can be soaked off later. The addition to the stem at the mortise must match the thickness of the pivot block. A small chisel will pick out the waste.

When a very narrow groove is required a cutter must be ground or filed to size from a small piece of square tool sheet.

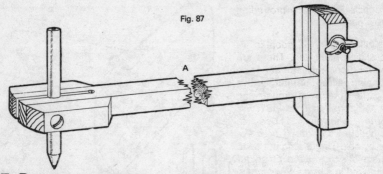

Fig. 87

87 Beam compasses

This excellent and virtually cost free tool is shown assembled at **A**. In constructing it, first machine an overlength piece of square section material, say 16 × 16mm ($\frac{5}{8} \times \frac{5}{8}$in). Cut off five pieces to make respectively, pieces **a**, **b**, **c** and **d**. All except **d** are sawn in half. The inside ends of **c** and **d** are finished quite square and all other ends are angled. Glue the **a**'s to the stem and **c** and **d** between the **b**'s using a short waxed block cut from the stem as a spacer. Hold the pieces together flat on a piece of polythene sheet. Drill a hole in end **B** for a pencil or ballpoint, the latter is often better, and then drill a small terminal hole of 3mm ($\frac{1}{8}$in) and a lateral hole for the clamp screw. A brass roundhead 12ga × 1½in is well suited for the cramp up. Drill half way at 6mm ($\frac{1}{4}$in). Drill the remaining distance at 3mm ($\frac{1}{8}$in). Saw the slot with a saw having a wide kerf. Screw up and test with the chosen pen

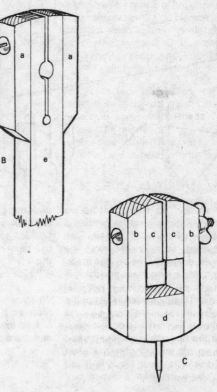

or pencil. File off any protruding screw point.

A similar routine is adopted for the sliding point unit. There are several possibilities for the clamping screw. Either put a clear hole halfway through and tap the other half $\frac{1}{4}$in BSW, or metric equivalent. Use a thumbscrew to tighten or make one by soldering a wing nut on to a piece of screwed rod. Or solder a wing nut to a brass woodscrew. Screw in a normal woodscrew first then replace with the one made up. Or drill clear holes right through and use a 5mm ($\frac{1}{4}$in) coach bolt with wing nut.

The point can be made by grinding up a piece of silver steel of about 3mm ($\frac{3}{32}$in) diameter. Clean up the whole job, lightly sand and finish either with a polyurethane varnish or teak oil.

87 Beam compasses, alternative design

The beam is a length of dowel 8mm ($\frac{5}{16}$in) or, better, 10mm ($\frac{3}{8}$in) diameter. A block is made for the point, a piece of 3mm ($\frac{1}{8}$in) silver steel, and similar blocks are made for pencil and ballpoint work. Woodscrews are quite adequate to clamp the blocks on to dowel and ballpoint. In cases where the centre point mark must not show, glue on a small wood block with a paper joint and pivot from this.

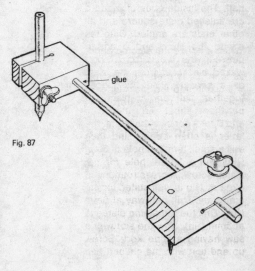

glue

Fig. 87

88 Spokeshave blade holders

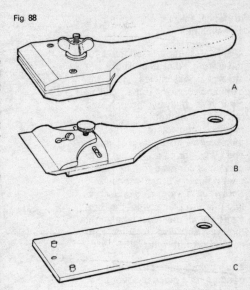

Fig. 88

The modern spokeshave blade is much too small to be hand held for sharpening. Two convenient holders are illustrated. The first, **A**, is of wood and is quite straightforward. The wing nut tightener is an improvement over a mere slot. Two small pins prevent the blade going in too far. They are in loose holes in the top and are driven into the bottom.

The second, **B**, is of metal, 3mm (⅛in) is quite suitable. A cutter is cramped in place and two holes are drilled through for the pegs which locate the cutter, which is held in place by the normal spokeshave wedge. A shaped handle can be filed up or a tang made to be driven into a turned wooden handle.

When a horizontal electric grinder is available the parallel sided version, **C**, is preferable as this will clamp into the tool holder in the manner of a plane iron.

89 Laminated mallets

The standard, commercially-produced mallet is not to every workers liking. Often the material is soft, wearing hollow very quickly. Handles may be unduly long and sometimes taper away from the head – the opposite to what is required. Cutting the deep tapered mortise, however,

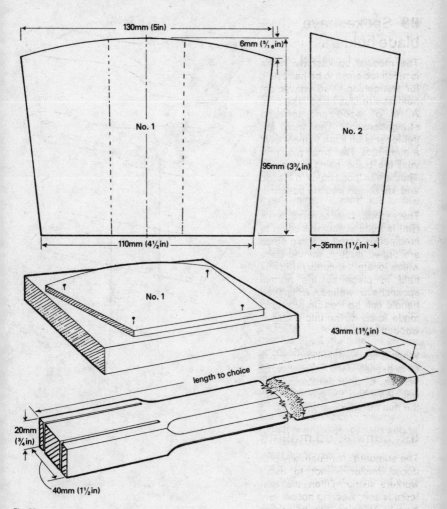

130mm (5in)

6mm (5⁄16in)

No. 1

No. 2

95mm (3¾in)

110mm (4½in)

35mm (1⅛in)

No. 1

43mm (1⅝in)

length to choice

20mm (¾in)

40mm (1½in)

Fig. 89

is what prevents most workers from making their own.

Good mallets for normal or special use can easily be made by lamination, the pieces being cut to size on the sawbench, using the template fence described on page 146. Two templates are required made from 6mm ($\frac{1}{4}$in) ply. The faces of the template should be marked clearly **A** and **B** respectively. Any good hardwood is suitable; beech, oak, elm, ash, walnut and tropical timbers have been used. This should be machined to one third of the desired mallet thickness, 20 to 25mm ($\frac{3}{4}$ to 1in) or even greater. The components are cut roughly over-size. Template 1 is pinned on, face **A** up and cut out using the template fence Fig. 160C. To cover slight inaccuracies this is repeated with face **B** up. Two pieces of template 2 are cut and one handle. Ideally this should be ash or hickory. The mallet head pieces are now glued together with a good, freshly-mixed, synthetic resin glue. They may be pinned with brass or bronze nails or dowelled to resist the tendency to slide, but this is not essential, being largely a matter of taste. While in the cramps wash out any glue from the mortise.

If the gluing up has been carefully done the minimum of cleaning up of the head will be necessary. One or two shavings from the handle will permit it to enter

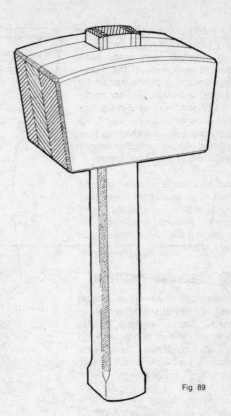

Fig. 89

the mortise but it will be found very loose at the top. Two carefully marked out and sawn wedges will secure the head. Slight shaping of the handle for comfort is best done after wedging with the head held in the vice and a slight chamfer round the head prevents the corners from splitting. A coat or two of varnish keeps the tool looking smart.

Out of a large number of such mallets no examples have been found with glue failure. Very careful planing, preferably by machine, and good fresh glue have ensured this.

90 Carvers' mallets

These mallets are not always easy to buy but are quite easy to make. Some workers prefer them for normal bench work as well as for carving. Many hardwoods are suitable for the heads, especially fruit woods. Small trees felled in the garden are particularly useful. The handle is short so almost any wood will do for this. Two sizes are shown and two common shapes. There are, of course, any number of variations. Heads are normally turned between centres but it is common to find the grain at right-angles to the shaft. The shaft is wedged but not glued.

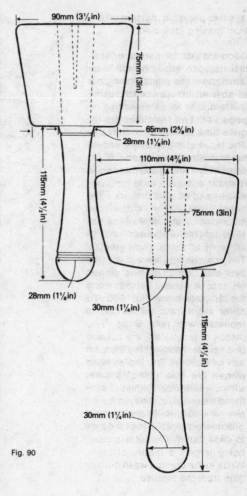

Fig. 90

91 Handscrews

These tools are much less common than they were a generation ago. Nevertheless they have several advantages over the much more numerous G cramps. They are lighter in weight, they do not damage the work and, of course, they can be made. Jaw length can vary between 300mm (12in) and 100mm (4in). They are usually square in section and are made from any close-grained hardwood. The screws can be of wood, if a wood screw box is available, or can be of bought metal screwed rod. The latter would be of a smaller size. The metal screws can be screwed, glued and even pinned into chisel-type handles and wood screws can be similarly fitted if it is required to cut out some of the woodturning.

It must be stressed that both the threaded holes are in the same jaw, in this illustration the lower one. In use the through screw makes the preliminary grip then the second shorter one screws into a cavity in the upper jaw thus increasing the pressure.

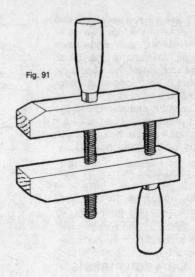

Fig. 91

92 Light cramps of fixed sizes

The weight of ironmongery on relatively small jobs is sometimes out of all proportion and in a home workshop or in a busy communal workshop a large number of cramps may not be available. These cramps are an attempt to solve the problem of weight and number. A typical use, glueing in drawer slip, is illustrated.

Any hardwood will do – beech being preferred. Small offcuts can be used up and a small saw-bench and drilling machine make light of the task. Coachbolts and wing nuts are preferred but is may be difficult to find coachbolts in imperial sizes or wing nuts in metric. In the absence of wing nuts, hexagon nuts and a tubular box spanner will have to be used. Beware of adding too much weight, 8 mm ($\frac{5}{16}$in) or even 6mm ($\frac{1}{4}$in) coachbolts are quite strong enough.

Face the jaws with adhesive plastic tape. This stops glue from sticking and is easily removed. The hole in the moving jaw should be slightly elongated with a rasp to give easy operation. The square hole for the coachbolt head will have to be cut. In a hardwood it will not be possible to force in the bolt.

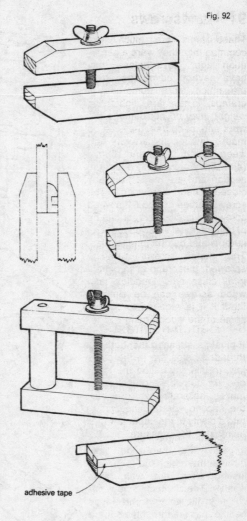

Fig. 92

adhesive tape

93 Light board cramps

The tool detailed at **A** was originally designed to be used as in **B** to prevent spelching or splitting off when planing end grain. It is lighter, more convenient and more effective than struggling with a heavy sash cramp. The hardwood block is slightly drilled to take the screw end. A refinement is to put a steel disc at the bottom of the hole to prevent wear.

Light boards can also be glued up, using two or three of these cramps as in **C**. Lengths can vary to suit the work most commonly done and 20mm (¾in) and 25mm (1in) capacities are probably the most convenient. Suggested dimensions are shown at **D**.

94 Bench holdfast

This is built on the same principle as the handscrew, Fig. 91, and operates through a very small hole in the benchtop, compared with the iron holdfasts, so can be arranged to work almost anywhere. A long coachbolt, or a fabricated equivalent, runs through the hardwood jaw, through the bench top to the adjusting wing nut with large washer. The clamping screw, secured in its wooden chisel-type handle, passes through a square nut let into the underside of the jaw. The bench top is protected, either by a hardwood or metal

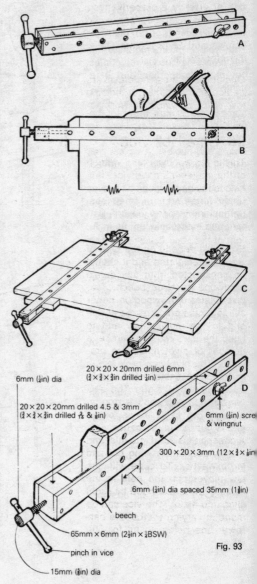

6mm (¼in) dia

20 × 20 × 20mm drilled 6mm
(¾ × ¾ × ¾in drilled ¼in)

20 × 20 × 20mm drilled 4.5 & 3mm
(¾ × ¾ × ¾in drilled 3/16 & ⅛in)

6mm (¼in) screw & wingnut

300 × 20 × 3mm (12 × ¾ × ⅛in)

6mm (¼in) dia spaced 35mm (1⅜in)

beech

65mm × 6mm (2½in × ¼BSW)

pinch in vice

15mm (⅝in) dia

Fig. 93

pad or else by a properly-made cramp foot. Average sizes would be 10 or 12mm ($\frac{3}{8}$ or $\frac{1}{2}$in) diameter screws and 35 × 28mm ($1\frac{3}{8}$ × $1\frac{1}{8}$in) for the jaw.

One or two of these holdfasts are particularly suitable for holding low relief carvings or work for power routing.

95 Small job vice

This is the woodworker's version of the engineer's hand vice. It is held in the bench vice and proves useful for all sorts of small jobs, particularly wooden jewelry, pattern and model making, as in **A**.

Sizes will depend on the type of work contemplated and it should be constructed from any dense hardwood such as beech. Two pivot plates of plywood or, better still, of brass are screwed at one end to the moving jaw and to keep the jaws roughly parallel a number of pivot holes are provided. The pivot can be a length of 3mm ($\frac{1}{8}$in) diameter rod, cranked at one end for a grip. The jaws can be lined with wood, leather or rubber. The fixed jaw is longer and is gripped in the bench vice. A coachbolt is fitted into this, and is provided with a wing nut and large washer. To cope with the jaw movement, the hole in the moving jaw is extended by slight filing into a slot. The vice can be made in varying widths, the narrower one being useful for fine work.

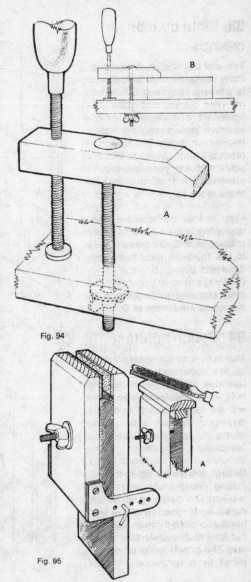

Fig. 94

Fig. 95

96 Vice clamps for sculpture

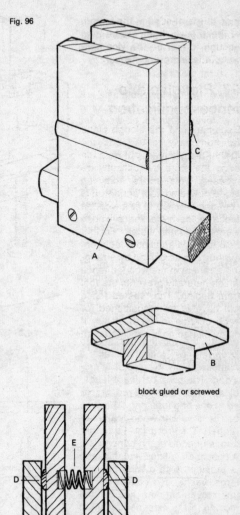

Fig. 96

The holding of sculpture, particularly of the flat back variety such as plaques, presents a holding problem if a sculptor's vice is not available. The device drawn at **A** is made of two jaws or chops of beech or similar hardwood of about 20mm (¾in). A block of about 25mm (1in) square and long enough to fit over the slide bars of the bench vice is glued to the bottom of one jaw. Its opposite face is slightly rounded and the other jaw is secured to it with well countersunk screws in overlarge holes, permitting some movement.

The block screwed or glued to the underside of the sculpture, **B**, should also be about 25mm (1in) thick and if glued, use a scotch (animal) glue with a paper joint. Rest the jaws of the clamp on the bench vice bars and in this position glue on two small strips to take the pressure near the top of the vice jaws, **C** and **D**. A spring, **E**, located in two shallow holes permits the jaws to open when the vice opens.

F shows a removable high vice jaw which fits over the normal vice jaw. 20mm (¾in) beech screwed to 13mm (½in) plywood is suitable for this pair of jaws. Assuming that 25mm (1in) blocks are fixed to the work, then a spacing block of slightly less

block glued or screwed

bench vice jaws

than this is needed at the bottom of these jaws. It should be long enough to rest on the vice bars without falling off or through.

97 Plough plane – fence modification

Beginners find the plough plane far from easy to use and the further the groove is cut from the edge the more the difficulty increases. This arises from the blade not being kept upright. It is common practice to fit a wooden fence to the metal fence whose increased depth helps. Further help towards an almost foolproof method can be gained by arranging a rebate in the wooden fence which naturally prevents the tool from tipping. The rebated fence will have to be repositioned for each change in depth of cut. If much ploughing is anticipated an adjustable stop can be fitted to the wooden fence.

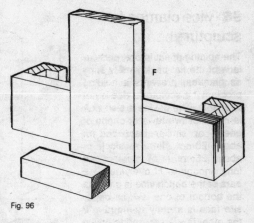

Fig. 96

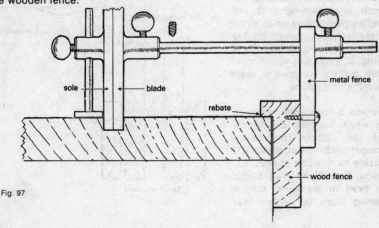

Fig. 97

98 Improved shooting board

The conventional shooting board suffers from several disadvantages which have been eliminated in this model. Beginners and the inexperienced are liable to cant over the plane cutting away part of the board and the planing stop, thus causing inaccuracies. Working against the planing stop (a very old fashioned and inefficient device anyway) does not give the stability obtained here by gripping in the bench vice. Once the plane has cut the smallest of rebates in the guides no further damage to the board is possible.

A packing piece of appropriate thickness makes sure that the cut takes place approximately in the centre of the blade. This packing piece can be replaced by false tables arranging for angles other than 90° to be cut. This board can be planned as left or right-handed and to take either the 50mm or 60mm (2in or 2⅜in) jack plane.

Fig.98

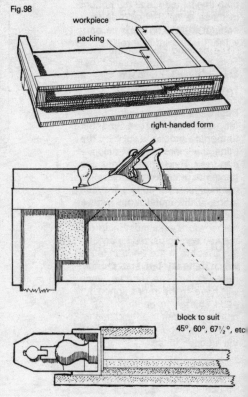

workpiece
packing

right-handed form

block to suit
45°, 60°, 67½°, etc

99 False tables for shooting board

The packing piece of the shooting board can be replaced by a false table, **A**, fitted with an angled block at 45° for mitring angles of rectangles, or 60° for the angles of hexagons, or 67½° for the angles of octagons. An alternative false table can be fitted with an adjustable stop, **B**. As the curved corner of this does not give efficient support to the workpiece it is necessary to interpose a parallel strip of hardwood.

100 False tables for angles other than 90°

Bevelling and edge jointing at angles other than 90°, as in coopered doors or stave-built turnery, can easily be achieved by false tables fitted to the basic shooting board. A number of these can be made from multi-ply or even chipboard supported by differing pairs of wedges. Drill a clearance hole through both the table and the wedge. Glue the wedge to the false table only and when tightening up the screw make sure that both the wedges and the table are pressed firmly against the sole of a plane, which is held in the working position.

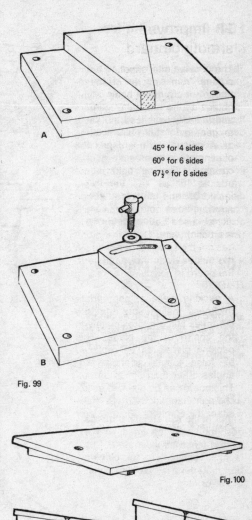

45° for 4 sides
60° for 6 sides
67½° for 8 sides

Fig. 99

Fig. 100

101 Improved mitre shooting board

This tool is an alternative to the traditional 'donkey's ear' shooting board. It offers the same advantages as the previous board. It can be firmly held, it cannot be damaged and retains its accuracy. Additionally the workpiece can be more conveniently held horizontally than sloping upwards at 45° as with the traditional board. Left or right-handed models can be constructed to suit a 50mm or 60mm (2in or 2⅜in) plane.

102 Shaped plane handle

The use of the plane on the shooting board is made easier by the use of a side handle. The side of the plane, left or right, can be tapped to take either a turned knob or a carved handle.

103

Either of the two shooting boards described may be fitted with a slotted fence as illustrated. This is most convenient for planing thin material truly parallel either at 90° or 45°.

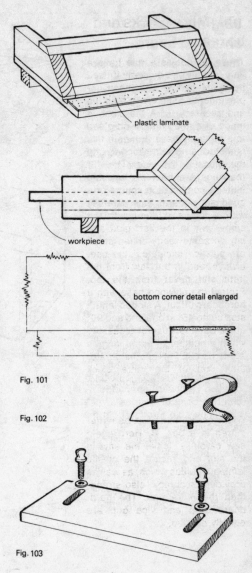

plastic laminate

workpiece

bottom corner detail enlarged

Fig. 101

Fig. 102

Fig. 103

104 Mitre blocks and boxes

Fig. 104

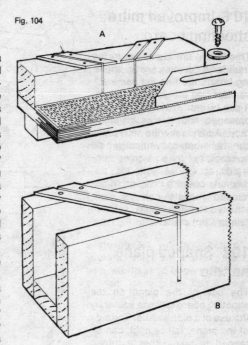

These do not as a rule have a very long life, particularly if used by many people and these improvements will prolong both life and accuracy. In **A** the block is made of a good hardwood glued to a multi-ply base. Beneath this is a stout strip with which to grip the block in the vice. The 45° markings are best made using either a combination square or a good set square. Saw carefully with a fine saw, then with the same saw in the kerf glue and pin on some ready-drilled strips of plastic laminate. In use, always feed in the saw from the front and never from the top. Protect the plywood base with a hardboard offcut. A slotted length stop cut to 45° at one end and 90° at the other is a useful accessory when a number of equal lengths are to be cut. For lengths greater than that of the mitre block cramp a stop to the workbench top.

Wider components can be better mitred in a box, **B**. Here again saw carefully, leave the saw in the slot and secure the plastic laminate guides which, as well as providing accuracy, also strengthen the mitre box. The hardboard strip and vice grip are equally needed.

105 A tool for mitred dovetails

The mitre saw cut on a dovetail needs to be cut very accurately the first time. Any paring back to fit will either leave a gap or necessitate cutting back the dovetails. This device is simply a hardwood block from 50 × 50mm (2 × 2in) material which has been grooved to take a piece of 13mm (½in) multi-ply which should project between 50–70mm (2–3in). Carefully saw the mitres with a thin saw and fit plastic laminate guides as described in Fig. 104.

To use, first cut the dovetails then position the joint carefully on the plywood beneath the saw slot. Small workpieces and the aid can both be gripped in the bench vice. Wider pieces, as in carcase work, should be held in the vice with the mitre aid cramped in place. Do not insert the saw from the top.

106 Hand planing thin strips

Thin strips of identical thickness, such as may be required for laminating, can be accurately produced by hand planing by means of a simple jig. This consists of a base-block, **A**, and two rebated side members, **B**. The space between the two rebates must just allow free movement of the chosen jack plane. **A** projects below **B**, to be held in the vice.

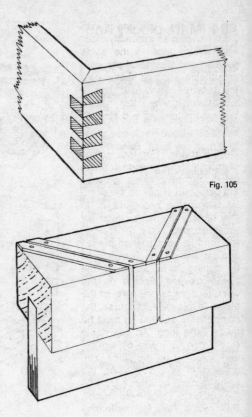

Fig. 105

The sides are glued and pinned in place using an assembly block with a true face in the plane position and a piece of ply, card or suitable spacing material of the required thickness. The illustration makes this clear. When complete, an end stop, **C**, is fitted.

Modifications For the making of stringings for inlaying or musical instrument making, grooves are ploughed or cut on the circular saw in the baseblock **A**. In this case there is no need for rebated sides. Very thin pieces will tend to buckle when planed against a stop. This is overcome by cutting away some of the baseblock and pinning on the workpiece below the level of the blade. In this case, of course, the components and the jig must be made extra long. An adjustable model can be made by slotting and screwing on the sides. The adjustment is made using the same method as when gluing on the sides to the simple model. Solid wood keys for reinforcing mitre joints, as described on page 24, can be produced in this manner.

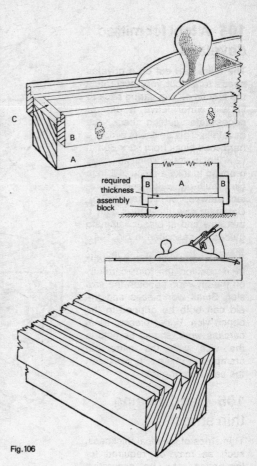

Fig. 106

107 Hand planing very small components

Very small components can best be planed by holding a plane upside down in the vice and pushing the workpiece over the blade. As this method gives every chance of shaving off the finger tips, a push stick is an advantage. Even better is this simple planing device. It consists of a hardwood base with a firmly secured handle. Guide pieces, thinner than the finished job, can be pinned or glued on so that they can be changed when the aid is used for another job.

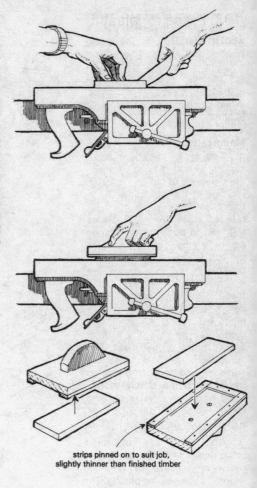

strips pinned on to suit job,
slightly thinner than finished timber

Fig. 107

108 Plane for plastic laminates

Although the normal bench plane can cope briefly with plastic laminates, a cutter ground to 25° and sharpened at 30° very quickly loses its edge. A more successful cutter can be made using a much less acute angle as at **A**. Grind the cutter in the normal way then turn it over and grind and hone the other side at 45°; this gives a section as in **B**. To prevent clogging, the cap iron should be sawn off at the end of the curve and filed smooth. The cap iron now serves only to move the blade. The other components remain unaltered. Assemble and use in the normal way. A little more pressure than usual will be necessary but not too heavy a cut should be used. This form of cutter will last much longer than the standard cutter, when used on laminate edges.

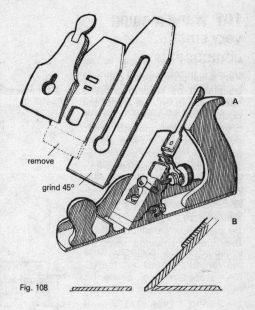

remove

grind 45°

Fig. 108

109 The hookdriver

Screwing a large number of hooks into correctly drilled pilot holes is certainly hard on the fingers. The use of pliers roughens the hook or, in the case of brassed or chromed hooks, damages the plating. The hookdriver made from any dense hardwood such as beech enables hooks to be put in in quantity and at speed with the minimum of effort and no discomfort.

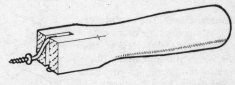

Fig. 109

110 Wooden jack plane

All the wood planes that follow are made by this built-up method, though they could be made in the solid if preferred. It is invariably advised that the end grain of the plane should look as shown at **A**, the medullary rays as nearly vertical as possible to prevent distortion. At the same time it has to be admitted that many old and perfectly satisfactory planes can be found in which this has been disregarded.

Wood Beech is the commonly accepted wood, preferably the red varieties. Hornbeam, maple, pear and cherry are common in Europe; boxwood and walnut are satisfactory though expensive. It would appear, then, that almost any good close-grained hardwood may be used.

Construction The centre block is first prepared accurately, generally 4mm (⅛in) thicker than the width of the intended blade. Follow the plans for the other dimensions. Length is kept a bit long. Make sure that the two sides are perfectly true, flat and parallel, and at right-angles to the sole. Prepare another piece the same length, of about 25mm (1in) thickness and of the width of the centre block plus 4mm (⅛in) or so. Plane both faces with great care and mark both with a face mark. From each face

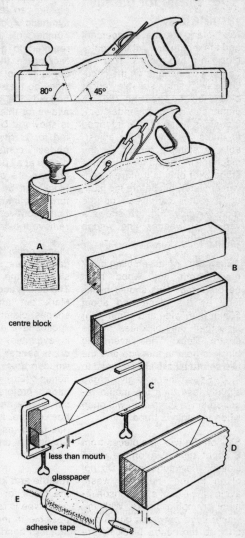

Fig. 110

gauge the thickness of the side pieces, **B**.

Next mark out the escapement and the mouth and cut the centre block into two pieces. This can be done by hand or on the circular saw using suitable angle blocks on the crosscut slide. A planer saw is recommended for a first-class finish. If it is intended to make the plane fully adjustable, a suitable recess for the mechanism should be cut at this stage. Not only is it more inconvenient later, but before the glue-up a router can clean up the recess nicely. Fig. 118 shows a variety of wedges and wedge fixing methods.

Assembly An assembling block made from any wood must be prepared. This should be as long as the plane and about 50mm (2in) wide and 13mm ($\frac{1}{2}$in) less than the thickness of the centre block. The assembling block is held in the vice and the two centre blocks are cramped to it, **C**. Space these to give a gap slightly less than the mouth required since the mouth will open when the sole is trued.

Saw off the two side pieces from **B** about 2mm ($\frac{1}{16}$in) on the waste side of the gauge lines. Do *not* plane to the line. This waste avoids the use of a lot of inconvenient cramping blocks. With the waste edge outwards glue up at once to the centre block before

any warping of the thin side pieces can take place, using a synthetic resin glue. A large number of G-cramps will be required to get a perfect joint. Nipping in the bench vice will certainly not do. Position the sides so that they project a little beyond the sole, their width allows for this. The arrangement is shown at **D** with cramps omitted for clarity. Make sure of a perfect contact between the pieces at all points. Once several cramps are on, the assembling block can be released and two further cramps added to the job. Leave for twenty-four hours, then remove the cramps.

Plane down the sides to their gauge lines and clean off the steps on the sole and the top. The sole is accurately trued later. Mark out and saw the side shapes, cleaning up with gouge, spokeshave and rasp. If a lathe is available, finish on a small drum sander, shown at **E**. The wooden drum is turned to about 50mm (2in) diameter. Glasspaper, preferably open coat, is cut to size and held on with adhesive tape. It is rather a bumpy ride but gives a first-class finish. Shape the ends and bevel the corners.

Handle and knob Now prepare the block for the handle. If the open type is required, it might be possible to incorporate a manufactured handle. This will be out of the question if the closed type as illustrated is chosen since the ramp on which the blade beds is continued up the handle for more support. Cut the mortise and fit the block to it. Shape the handle according to preference, having due regard to accommodating the mechanism if it is to be fitted. The closed handles are fitted with a slight projection which can be cleaned off with a small block plane so that the blade fits snugly.

The design for the front knob can be evolved to suit individual requirements, glue the knob in as the last phase of the whole job.

Cutter If the cutting units are standard components as used in Record and Stanley planes, the vital factor in fitting this unit is to position the lever cap screw exactly. To do this bind the cap iron and the cutter together in their working position with adhesive tape and remove the cap iron screw. Place the lever cap in its working position and bind this also. Stand the plane on a flat surface and insert the blade. Through the hole in the lever cap scribe the centre for the lever cap screw. If there is to be no adjustment mechanism remove the lever cap only, replace the cap iron and cutter and, through the hole for the cap iron screw, mark its centre. On this centre, with a forstner bit for preference, bore a hole to accommodate the cap iron screw. The lever cap screw may be a No. 12 round-head steel wood screw. An improvement is to make a brass bush from a short length of $\frac{1}{2}$in Whitworth screwed rod. This can be bored centrally with a $\frac{7}{16}$in drill, then tapped to take a $\frac{1}{4}$in machine screw with round head. Equivalent metric threads are equally suitable.

Finishing The most satisfactory method is to clean up the plane and give a few coats of either clear cellulose or clear french polish thinned 50/50. Rub off the nibs with waxed steel wool. True up the sole with the cutting unit in place, cutter withdrawn. Ensure that the lever cap screw is tight enough. If there is no mechanism the screw must be tighter than is the case in an iron plane. Test with straight-edge and winding strips. Wipe the sole periodically with raw linseed oil.

Adjustment by hammer is apt to damage a nicely-built plane, so where possible it is advisable to fit a striking button. This is equally effective whether placed on top at the front, or on the end at the rear. Boxwood or rosewood are suitable woods.

Test the completed plane on mild timber first, making sure to try it on a wide face as well as on a narrow edge. Keep the mouth as fine as possible but remedy clogging by gently paring or filing the mouth wider. An adjustable mouth, which can be fitted to the existing plane or incorporated into a future one, is described in Fig. 111; also several varieties of mechanism, all of which can be made with basic hand tools.

111 Jack plane with simple mechanism

This plane is built up in the same way as the non-adjustable version. The two centre blocks **A** and **B** are glued between side blocks. Before gluing, the front block, **B**, has a recess cut out to take the sliding mouth, **C**. The main block is passed over the circular saw to give a groove to take the adjusting arm, **H**. This is joined again on top by a capping piece, **F**. This piece is set back slightly from the bed to make room for the lateral lever **G**. This is identical to the lateral levers on the metal planes. The greater length of this plane makes it possible to fit the simpler mechanism. The adjustment screw, **J**, and wheel, **K**, are placed as far forward as possible, if necessary by cutting a slight recess in the block. M6 or ½in BSF are suitable threads. If left-hand threads can be cut this will preserve the convention of

Fig. 111

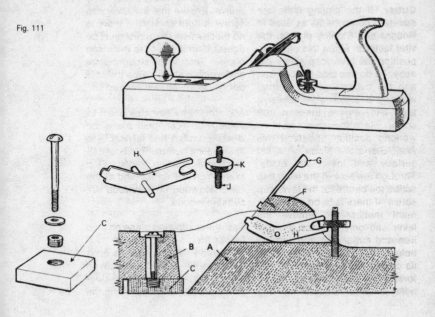

clockwise rotation increasing the cut. A cardboard template of the adjusting arm **H** should be carefully drawn and cut out. Drill the pivot hole 3mm ($\frac{1}{8}$in) and try out the pattern, correcting where necessary. Using the template make the arm itself using 4 or 5mm ($\frac{3}{16}$in) mild steel. Fit the arm, put in the lever cap, screw, assemble all the parts and check that the mechanism works properly.

The sliding mouth, **C**, has a metal insert or nut fitted to it. This may be screwed in or glued with epoxy resin. The locking screw operates through a slotted hole and holds the mouth firmly in place. When this operates successfully, screw it firmly in place and plane the sole true. Lastly fit the handles.

112 Adjustable wood smoothing plane

This is a delightful plane to use. Many readers will find the rear handle is well worth the work it involves. The 50mm (2in) size seems the most satisfactory, though a 45mm (1$\frac{3}{4}$in) could well be made to satisfy some special need. The use of a 60mm (2$\frac{3}{8}$in) cutter would produce a massive plane of doubtful advantage. The plane is fitted with an effective adjustment mechanism which can easily be made at home.

A closed handle is fitted and, as no satisfactory handle is manufactured, one will have to be made. Try to finish it at 25mm (1in). A thin handle, out of stuff 25mm (1in) sawn, is unpleasant to hold. Make a full-size drawing of the handle on cardboard which can then be cut out and used as a template. A similar template may be found useful for the body. The home-made sanding drum described on page 84 is very helpful used on the body but there is no short cut to making the handle. Any means are justifiable and they may include gouges, rasps, files and narrow scrapers made from hacksaw blades. These will eventually produce a shape that suits. Before fixing it, do not forget to cut back the handle to accommodate the lateral lever and groove it to take the spindle.

The body is built up with two sides glued to the two centre blocks in much the same way that the jack plane described on page 84 and, in fact, a similar assembly jig can be rigged up. Resin glue should be used. Whatever finish has been chosen, give several coats before gluing in the handle. This prevents the glue, which oozes from the handle joint, from sticking to the surface.

The adjustment mechanism follows. In making it ensure that the length of the spindle and the lateral lever is such that the plane will take a new full-length cutter. According to its size and style, the top of the handle may have to be modified to accommodate the brass knob.

Mechanism This can be made with hand tools by any woodworker of average skill. It can be fitted to this plane, or it can be added to an existing plane. The whole device is made from bright mild steel, except for its brass knob. The assembled parts seen from the side and above are shown at **A**. The individual pieces at **B**. The base plate consists of a strip 20mm ($\frac{3}{4}$in) by 4mm ($\frac{1}{8}$in) approximately 75mm (3in) long. From a length of 15 × 15mm ($\frac{1}{2} \times \frac{1}{2}$in) steel cut three blocks 20mm ($\frac{3}{4}$in) long. File one down to a thickness of just under 13mm ($\frac{7}{16}$in). This block and one other are fixed to the base strip 45mm ($1\frac{3}{4}$in) apart. They may be brazed, riveted with 4mm ($\frac{1}{8}$in) diameter rod or screwed from beneath. The plate is next bored and countersunk to take two No. 6 wood screws. Having marked out the centres, screw this assembly to a right-angled block, **C**, making sure that it is vertical. Cramp the centre moving block exactly beneath the top fixed block and, using a drill press or mechanically-held drill and 5mm ($\frac{3}{16}$in) bit, drill through them all. Remove the moving block and put a 6mm ($\frac{1}{4}$in) drill through the top block. Now reverse the whole and on

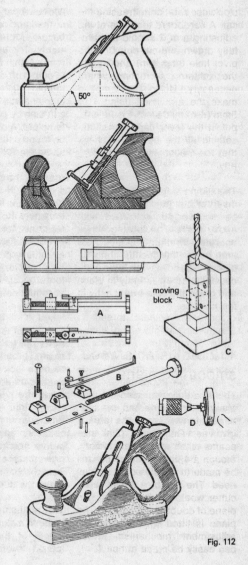

Fig. 112

the same axis drill the bottom block with any drill between 1·5mm ($\frac{1}{16}$in) and 3mm ($\frac{1}{8}$in). Reverse again and bore into the inner side of the lower block, on this pilot hole, 6mm ($\frac{1}{4}$in) deep using a 6mm ($\frac{1}{4}$in) drill.

The centre sliding block is drilled on top and tapped to take a 5mm ($\frac{3}{16}$in) diameter peg. With this firmly in position again clear the original 5mm ($\frac{3}{16}$in) hole and tap with $\frac{1}{4}$in BSF. Whitworth will do at a pinch but will not give so fine an adjustment. The normal thread will require an anti-clockwise turn to increase the cut. To obtain the conventional clockwise rotation a left-handed thread must be used. Left-handed taps and dies can be readily obtained from any reputable tool dealer.

To make the spindle, thread a 135mm (5in) length of $\frac{1}{4}$in diameter for 55mm (2$\frac{1}{4}$in). Take care if unpractised to start the thread squarely. Return to the body and on top of the upper block, drill and tap at $\frac{1}{8}$in to meet the $\frac{1}{4}$in through hole. Do not put through the plug tap but leave the thread tight. File a $\frac{1}{8}$in keyway round the spindle at the appropriate place. This can be done in the chuck of a woodturning lathe. Assemble and test for smooth working with a $\frac{1}{8}$in screw in place.

Make the lateral lever from a strip of 10mm × 1·5mm ($\frac{3}{8}$in × $\frac{1}{16}$in) stock. Drill a 3mm ($\frac{1}{8}$in)

diameter hole near one end for the rivet and another 13mm ($\frac{1}{2}$in) from it for the pivot screw. Countersink each appropriately. From a 12mm ($\frac{7}{16}$in) diameter rod, previously drilled at $\frac{1}{8}$in cut off a 1·5mm ($\frac{1}{16}$in) slice. Rivet on this stud, then assemble. File the end of the pivot screw until it holds the lever firm yet does not foul in the keyway. The lever cap securing screw hole is now drilled in the lower block. A $\frac{1}{4}$in BSF or Whitworth round-head screw will do the job. Now assemble in the plane with a full-length cutter to see where to cut off the spindle and crank the lateral lever. The position in the plane of the lever cap screw is of importance as this controls the position of the lever cap. If this comes too low the mouth will clog.

Make the knob from a brass disc 25 × 8mm (1 × $\frac{5}{16}$in) thick. Drill a 5mm ($\frac{3}{16}$in) hole in the centre and tap $\frac{1}{4}$in. Thread some $\frac{1}{4}$in diameter rod on a lock nut, and screw on the disc as at **D**. Turn up in the chuck of a woodturning lathe or electric drill. A hand turning tool can be ground from an old file; the cutting angle for brass is 90°. Twelve notches filed round the edge give an adequate grip. Thread the spindle end and screw on the knob and then wedge or pin it securely. Cut off the lateral lever 10mm ($\frac{3}{8}$in) past the bend and round its tip.

Cut off the peg at a suitable

length in the cap iron slot and ensure that the housing in the plane body is deep enough, and that the lateral lever does not foul on the wood anywhere. Adjust the lever cap screw to a convenient degree of tightness. Sharpen and test, starting on some mild softwood.

The adjustment mechanism could also be fitted to the jack plane.

113 Adjustable scraper plane

This type of plane has the advantage over the spokeshave type in that having a longer sole, it is not so liable to plane hollow. Also, being wooden, it slides more sweetly. Similar planes, called veneer planes and made of iron, were available in at least two models many years ago. The present plane, though fulfilling a similar purpose, is not a mere reproduction of them. The need for the wooden sole must have been felt before, since at least one model of scraper plane had provision for the attachment of a wooden sole. This plane can be made with only basic hand tools though it is a great help if the escapement is cut with a fine circular saw.

Centre stock Prepare as described on page 84 with a width of 63mm (2½in). Mark out and cut

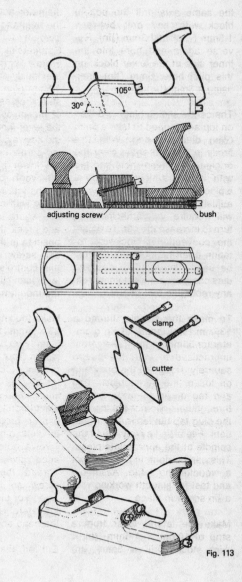

Fig. 113

the escapement. The angle on the rear section is a forward leaning angle of 105°; the front angle is 30°. A small step cut on the front block helps to keep the mouth small and at the same time helps to reduce the chance of shavings piling up behind the clamp bar and causing clogging.

Next bore the 6 mm ($\frac{1}{4}$in) hole for the long adjusting screw. Locate the centres and bore from each end. A lathe is a great help towards accuracy here. This screw can run through a brass bush as the drawing shows. It is made from a piece of $\frac{1}{4}$in Whitworth screwed brass rod. This is drilled centrally and tapped at $\frac{1}{8}$in. Alternatively a brass $\frac{1}{4}$in nut can be sunk into the bed behind the blade. The clamp screws can run in grooves cut in the centre block before the glue-up. Otherwise, they too may be bored if accurately marked at each end.

The sides are prepared in the usual manner and glued on as soon as possible after they have been sawn out to minimise the chance of their warping. Clean up and fit a manufactured handle. Glue it in place. Turn the knob according to individual taste and fix with glue. Make sure that it comfortably clears the blade.

Metal work The clamp bar is a piece of 15 × 3mm ($\frac{1}{2}$ × $\frac{1}{8}$in) mild steel, drilled and tapped $\frac{1}{8}$in Whitworth. All three screws are easily

made from brass by soldering $\frac{1}{8}$in screwed rod into a tube of an inside diameter of $\frac{1}{8}$in, all three need a sawcut for the screwdriver and the two clamp screws require a brass washer each.

The blade itself can either be a manufactured scraper blade, or made from a really heavy gauge cabinet scraper. The latter are particularly hard, but they can be filed and sawn; they are very hard on hacksaw blades. In some cases it may be worth softening the blade and subsequently re-hardening. Sharpen the blade with a file, and then oilstone it at 45° as described on page 59. Burnish over the edge and then stand the plane on a flat surface, drop in the blade and tighten up the clamps.

A fine cut will probably be obtained without the use of the adjusting screw and this is the method which should be aimed at, keeping the adjusting screw in reserve to increase the cut. The more the cutter is bent by the adjusting screw, the narrower will be the shavings. In operation, try to produce several fine shavings rather than a few thick ones. Cut parallel to the grain but hold at an angle to get a skew cut. Occasionally wipe the sole with a drop of raw linseed oil, otherwise maintenance is unnecessary.

114 Compass plane

The compass plane, for working shallow curves, is built up in the same way as the other laminated planes. The model with a sole curved in length only is quite straightforward. A plane curved in width also, presents a slight problem. Such a plane might be used, for example, to clean up a dished chair seat. The curved end to the blade necessitates a curved mouth slot. This is best achieved after glue-up and before shaping by chopping out a recess in front of the blade and fitting in a block as for remouthing a plane. Keep the mouth extra fine and, after shaping the sole, carefully pare or file away the block to give a fine mouth matching the blade shape.

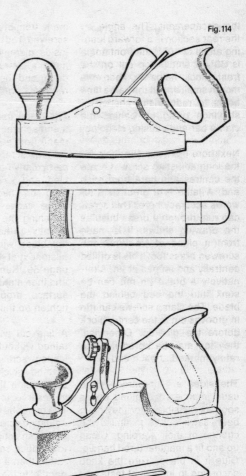

Fig. 114

115 Toothing plane

This tool, once bordering on extinction is now increasingly used to roughen the ground not only in preparation for veneering but also for plastic laminates. This handled version is much more convenient to use than the coffin-shaped model. The laminated construction is the same as that of the planes described earlier. Any of the blade securing methods is suitable and a good tool dealer can still supply toothing blades. The pitch of the blade should be 85°.

Fig. 115

116 Improved router

The addition of the levelling foot greatly increases the scope of this router by allowing it to work on such features as oversize tenons and rebates as shown in **A**. The basic construction from **B** is straightforward, it is made from 25mm (1in) beech or other dense hardwood. Cut out and bore the base then shape the block and glue it on. Drill the block for the clamp bolt 10mm (⅜in) then chop a shallow square recess of 13mm (½in) for the head. Cut a shallow housing of 6mm (¼in) in the base for the cutter. Drill the ends and glue in four nylon knock-down fittings. Drill holes of 16mm (⅝in) then turn the handles to suit. Varnish the body and handles with three coats of polyurethene varnish and then glue in the handles. The levelling foot, **D**, is simply a slotted hardwood block secured with two round-head screws with big washers at either end as required.

The shank of the cutter, **E**, is made from 6mm (¼in) square mild steel with a round tenon filed on the end. The cutters themselves are filed from tool steel. Drill and countersink then rivet and braze together. Harden and then temper to light brown, see page 204.

The clamp bolt, **C**, is turned or filed from a piece of 13mm (½in) square mild steel and threaded 10mm (⅜in). Drill and file a hole

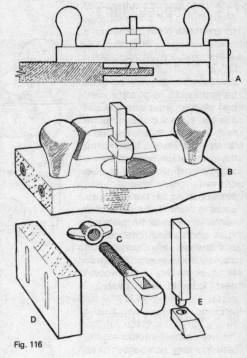

Fig. 116

for a loose fit on the cutter shank. A large wing nut and washer secure it through the block.

117 Shoulder plane

A satisfactory shoulder plane can be made with hand tools and a drill without great effort or skill. The two sides are roughly cut out from 3mm ($\frac{1}{8}$in) mild steel and two of the holes are drilled so that they can be bolted together and filed to shape. A sole, of 10 × 10mm ($\frac{3}{8} \times \frac{3}{8}$in) steel is held in position using the two bolts and a packing piece. The three components are then drilled, countersunk and riveted together. This is followed by the 6mm ($\frac{1}{4}$in) strip above the wedge. The wood filling, preferably of rosewood, is next inserted and riveted in place. The assembly is now filed up true, drawfiled and finished with emery. The blade (of 3mm ($\frac{1}{8}$in) or 2mm ($\frac{3}{32}$in) tool steel) is filed to shape and hardened and tempered. (See details on page 204.) The wedge completes the job. Give great care in filing up the mouth, which must stay as fine as possible. A suitable length is 125mm (5in).

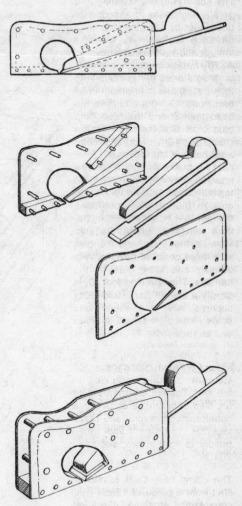

Fig. 117

118 Alternative wedges for wooden planes

Patterns **A**, **B** and **C** can be made either from a dense hardwood into which has been let a brass nut, or by sawing out from a solid piece of metal (brass looks best), or from a simple aluminium casting which is well within the capacity of a school or college workshop. **A** pivots on a large round-head woodscrew as the cap screw, **B** notches on to a steel pin, permanently fixed into the plane sides and **C** is best as a casting. This pivots on a removable pin which passes through two brass pivots glued into the plane sides. One pivot is threaded, the other has a clear hole. **D** is a hammer-adjusted, wooden wedge operating against a pivoting wooden bar. To ensure a really precise fit of the wedge on the blade it is essential that the bar should not be glued but left to move freely.

119 Dowel cutters

Dowels are seldom used singly, one generally requires a number of identical sizes. Two devices are shown for hand sawing. The long holes should be a fraction over the nominal size of the dowel to give an easy fit.

Device **A** will cut four standard sizes. Grip it in the bench vice and feed in a length of dowel

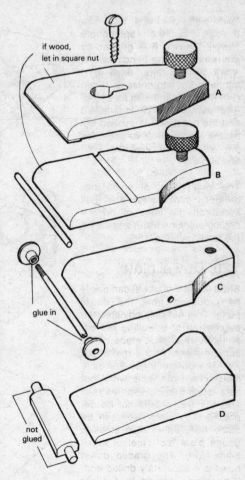

if wood,
let in square nut

A

B

glue in

C

not
glued

D

Fig. 118

flush with one end and saw
through at the appropriate
sawcut. Device **B** is gripped by
the rebates in the bench vice. A
small pin of, say, 3mm (⅛in)
diameter fits into holes at 10mm
(½in) intervals and acts as a stop.
After each cut the pin is removed
and the cut dowel is pushed out
by the length of dowelling. The
pin is replaced and the next
dowel cut.

The long holes, or small preparatory pilot holes, are best
bored on the lathe or on the
drilling machine using a spike on
the table, see Fig. 156.

120 Dowel plate

Short lengths of dowel can easily
be produced from the dowel
plate. This not only obviates the
purchasing of dowelling but enables dowels to be made of the
same material as the rest of the
job. The dowels made are quite
satisfactory for joint work but
long lengths to be used as rails
and spindles should not be ex-
pected. The plate itself can be
made from either mild steel or
gauge plate tool steel of about
8mm (5⁄16in). The graded dowel
holes are accurately drilled and,
if possible, reamed to a slight
taper and four screw holes drilled
and countersunk. If made of tool
steel the piece is hardened and
tempered. If of mild steel it is
case hardened. See details on
page 204.

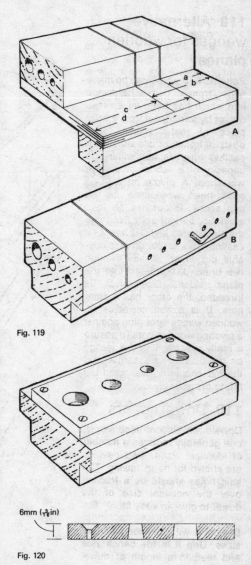

Fig. 119

6mm (5⁄16in)

Fig. 120

A hardwood baseblock is made with rebates which fit over the vice jaws. Holes are drilled to correspond with those in the plate but these are made larger to give clearance to the dowels. The plate is screwed to the base.

To make a dowel, roughly plane the wood to an octagonal section before driving it through a hole of larger size than is required. Then use successively smaller holes until the finished size is obtained. Drive only with a mallet to avoid damage to the cutting corner and finish the drive if necessary with a wooden punch.

121 Dowel groover

Dowels require a groove to enable excess glue to escape. A hardwood block of about 15mm (⅝in) thickness is drilled to take the common sizes of dowels used. A gauge 8 steel woodscrew is arranged as shown for each hole and regulated to give the required size of groove. The block is held on the open vice and the dowels are knocked through, either with a mallet or with a hammer and a wooden punch.

122 Dowelling aids

A shows a tool intended for the dowelling of narrow components, for example legs and rails or narrow flat frames. For a few jobs, a hardwood block and a

Fig. 121

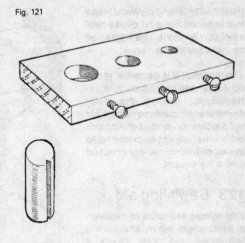

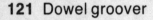

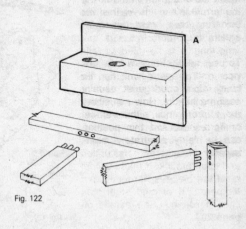

Fig. 122

plastic laminate or plywood fence is adequate. For a lot of use mild steel can be used. The bores can be case hardened.

The model at **B** is generally made up for a particular job. It is intended for jointing the wider members of carcase constructions either in wood or chipboard. Both must be firmly cramped to the work and the larger checked with a try square.

123 Saw filing aid

This simple aid helps to maintain a fixed angle when sharpening handsaws and also makes it easier to maintain an angle after a break in filing. A good handle is required preferably with a brass ferrule. A second ferrule fits snugly on this, but must turn freely. Into this is screwed a metal rod of about 75mm (3in). If the ferrule is thin it is worth silver soldering on a brass nut to increase the thread.

To use, set up the saw in a saw vice and press down the file firmly into a good gullet, usually near the handle. Now adjust the rod, to preference, either vertical or horizontal, and this position can be fairly accurately maintained.

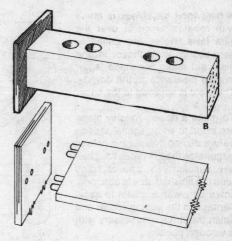

Fig. 122

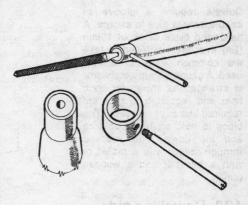

Fig. 123

124 Wood screw gauge

The principle of using a screw to join two pieces of wood is very simple but often wrongly carried out. The hole in the upper piece of wood known as the clearance hole should be as small as possible, yet the screw should be free to turn in it by finger grip. Too small a hole adds friction, making the screwing operation harder, without any gain in efficiency. The hole in the lower piece has a diameter which is that of the core of the screw. This is necessary because unlike a drill, a screw is not capable of removing wood. The core then fits into this pilot hole and the threads bite into the sides. The clearance hole may or may not be countersunk.

This simple device enables the correct clearance or pilot drill to be selected in an instant from either a millimetre or a fractional inch drill set, obviating the use of tables and reference books. A hardwood block, beech for example, is prepared to size and three rows of holes are drilled in it. Two rows are pilot holes and one is clearance holes. Screw in short specimen screws into the centre row so that all the heads stand up about 6mm ($\frac{1}{4}$in). A range from 14 to 2 gauge is generally enough. Brass-headed screws look better and resist

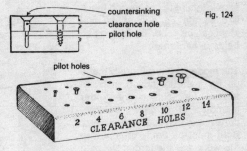

Fig. 124

corrosion. Number the screws with a felt-tipped marker.

In use simply identify the screw's gauge if not known by inverting head upon head and select drills to fit the corresponding holes in the block. Finally select a screwdriver whose blade width fits the screw slot exactly.

SCREW	2	4	6	8	10	12	14
CLEARANCE HOLE	$\frac{5}{64}$ inch 2mm	$\frac{7}{64}$ 3	$\frac{9}{64}$ 3·5	$\frac{11}{64}$ 4	$\frac{13}{64}$ 5	$\frac{15}{64}$ 5·5	$\frac{1}{4}$ 6·5
PILOT HOLE		$\frac{5}{64}$ 2	$\frac{5}{64}$ 2	$\frac{3}{32}$ 2·5	$\frac{7}{64}$ 3	$\frac{1}{8}$ 3	$\frac{9}{64}$ 3·5